Hebrews
Part 1: Chapters 1-8

An 11-Lesson Study Containing

Weekly Commentary

and

Daily Study Questions

Commentary by
Jean W. Randall

Daily Study Questions by

Kathy Rowland

JOY OF LIVING
BIBLE STUDIES

Published by Joy of Living Bible Studies

For a free catalog please contact us at:

    800-999-2703 or 805-650-0838
    website: www.joyofliving.org
    e-mail: info@joyofliving.org

This material was previously published as *Hebrews* (contained both Parts 1 and 2) © 2009.

ISBN   1-932017-72-0
          978-1-932017-72-4

About Joy of Living

For over 50 years Joy of Living has been effectively establishing individuals around the world in the sound, basic study of God's Word.

Evangelical and interdenominational, Joy of Living reaches across denominational and cultural barriers, enriching lives through the simple, pure truths of God's inspired Word, the Bible.

Studies are flexible, suited for both formal and informal meetings, as well as for personal study. Each lesson contains historical background, commentary and a week's worth of personal application questions, leading readers to discover fresh insights into God's Word. Courses covering many books in both the Old and New Testaments are available. Selected courses are also available in several foreign languages. Contact the Joy of Living office for details.

Joy of Living Bible Studies was founded by Doris W. Greig in 1971 and has grown to include classes in nearly every state in the Union and many foreign countries.

Table of Contents

How to Use Joy of Living Materials

This unique Bible study series may be used by people who know nothing about the Bible, as well as by more knowledgeable Christians. Each person is nurtured and discipled in God's Word, and many develop a personal relationship with Jesus Christ as they study.

Joy of Living is based on the idea that each person needs to open the Bible and let God speak to them by His Holy Spirit, applying the Scripture's message to their needs and opportunities, their family, church, job, community, and the world at large.

Only a Bible is needed for this study series. While commentaries may be helpful, it is not recommended that people consult them as they work through the daily study questions. It is most important to allow the Holy Spirit to lead them through the Bible passage and apply it to their hearts and lives. If desired, additional commentaries may be consulted after answering the questions on a particular passage.

The first lesson of a series includes an introduction to the study, plus the first week's daily study questions. Some questions are simple, and some are deeper for those who are more advanced.[1] The individual works through the Bible passages each day, praying and asking God's guidance in applying the truth to their own life. (The next lesson will contain the commentary on the Bible passage being covered in the study questions.)

To Use in a Group Setting:

After the daily personal study of the passage has been completed, the class gathers in a small group, where they pray together and discuss what they have written in response to the questions about the passage, clarifying problem areas and getting more insight into the passage. The small group/discussion leader helps the group focus on biblical truth, and not just on personal problems. The student is the only person who sees their own answers and shares only what they feel comfortable sharing.

After small groups meet for discussion and prayer, they often gather in a large group meeting where a teacher gives a brief lecture covering the essential teaching of the Bible passage that was studied during the prior week and discussed in the small groups. The teacher may clarify the passage and challenge class members to live a more committed daily life.

At home, the student begins the next lesson, which contains commentary notes on the prior week's passage and questions on a new Scripture passage.

---

1. Challenge questions are optional for those who want to dig deeper or write their personal opinion. The Personal questions are between the individual doing the study and God. Those answers may be shared in class only if the individual would like to.

Do You KNOW You Have Eternal Life?

Your condition...

For all have sinned and fall short of the glory of God. (Romans 3:23)
But your iniquities (sins) have separated you from your God. (Isaiah 59:2)
For the wages of sin is death. (Romans 6:23)

There is help...

For Christ died for sins once for all, the righteous for the unrighteous, to bring you to God. (1 Peter 3:18)
The gift of God is eternal life in Christ Jesus our Lord. (Romans 6:23)

What do I do?...

Repent, then, and turn to God, so that your sins may be wiped out. (Acts 3:19)
Believe in the Lord Jesus, and you will be saved. (Acts 16:31)

You CAN know...

He who has the Son has life; he who does not have the Son of God does not have life. I write these things to you who believe in the name of the Son of God so that you may know that you have eternal life. (1 John 5:12-13)

If you would like to make the decision today to repent and trust Christ as your Savior, either for the first time or as a re-commitment of your life, you may want to pray a prayer similar to this one:

Lord Jesus, I admit that I am a sinner. Please forgive my sins. Thank You for dying on the cross for me, and for coming alive again. I accept Your gifts of forgiveness and eternal life. I place my life in Your hands. I want to be Yours forever. Thank you for loving me so much. In Your Name I pray. Amen.

Hebrews
Lesson 1

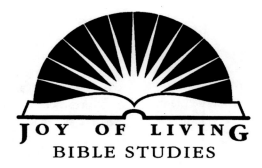

JOY OF LIVING
BIBLE STUDIES

Introduction

The letter to the Hebrews affords an enriching experience in the study of the Book of Books. With the Holy Spirit as your guide, you will find in the book of Hebrews wisdom and warning, as well as eternal truths that provide a pattern for practical Christian living. Hebrews is a great book; its teachings plumb the depths of the riches of God's Word.

You can approach the study of Scripture in different ways. Some people flit here and there in the Bible, hitting a few favorite verses, just skimming the surface but never letting God's Word become an integral part of their lives. Others spend much time cataloging facts of the Bible, but the knowledge stored in their minds never reaches their hearts, because they don't make room for the Lord in their lives. Others, however, read carefully and with the intent of letting God change their lives through His Word. These are the people who truly benefit spiritually from their time spent with the Bible.

As you begin this study of the Letter to the Hebrews, determine to give God your best time each day to read and meditate on His Word. The psalmist wrote, "The precepts of the LORD are right, giving joy to the heart. The commands of the LORD are radiant, giving light to the eyes. The fear of the LORD is pure, enduring forever. The ordinances of the LORD are sure and altogether righteous. They are more precious than gold, than much pure gold; they are sweeter than honey, than honey from the comb" (Psalm 19:8-10). Pray that your mind and heart will be filled with the honey of the Word of God. Pray that the Holy Spirit will enlighten you and give wisdom for your daily life (see Colossians 1:9-10). May He also enable you to share the sweetness and richness of His Word as your life touches people around you.

Author and Date

The authorship of Hebrews has been debated since early times without conclusive results. Though many believe that the thoughts are Paul's, the language and composition are unlike his other letters. Phrases such as "it has been written," and "the Scripture says," often used by Paul, do not appear in Hebrews. The *Expositors Bible Commentary* notes, "When [Hebrews] was accepted as part of the New Testament, this was partly at least because contemporaries held Paul to be the author. This view, however, appears to rest on no reliable evidence but rather to be a deduction from the facts that Paul was a prolific writer of epistles and that Hebrews is a noble writing that must have had a distinguished author. But both the language and thought forms are unlike those of Paul. The Greek is polished; Paul's is rugged, though vigorous."[1]

Origen, a third century scholar, concluded, "Only God knows surely who wrote Hebrews." Of one thing we can be reasonably certain: the writer was probably a Jew, thoroughly familiar with the law and prophetic writings. Some have attributed the writing to Barnabas or Apollos. Barnabas was a Jew of the priestly tribe of Levi (see Acts 4:36) who became a close friend of Paul's after Paul's conversion. Under the guidance of the Holy Spirit, the church at Antioch commissioned Barnabas and Paul for the work of evangelism and sent them off on the first missionary journey (see Acts 13:1-4).[2]

Apollos was a cultured, scholarly Jew from Alexandria, who is described in Acts 18:24-28 as learned, with a thorough knowledge of the Scriptures, and one who enthusiastically preached and taught in the synagogue. That his teaching methods differed from Paul's may account for the faction within the Corinthian church whose slogan was, "I am of Apollos" (see 1 Corinthians 1:12). Both Barnabas and Apollos were closely associated with Paul, which may be the explanation for the similarities as well as the differences, if in fact one of these two men wrote Hebrews.

The time of writing was apparently shortly before 70 A.D., when Roman armies destroyed the temple in Jerusalem. The author of Hebrews says nothing about the destruction of the temple, but leaves the impression that the Jewish sacrificial system, with its ministry of priests and all that that involved, was a continuing reality (see Hebrews 9:6-9).

Reason for Writing

Love for his Hebrew brothers and the Holy Spirit's guidance (see 2 Timothy 3:16-17) moved the author to write this message of love and earnest pleading. He was concerned that many had not grasped the full meaning of Christianity and were not growing spiritually. The letter is a warning for the Hebrews to pay closer attention to the things of the Lord and not to turn back, so that they would not drift away from Him. The author wanted to enlighten the Hebrew believers by explaining Christianity in the light of the Old Testament.

1. Frank E. Gaebelein, editor. *The Expositor's Bible Commentary* (Grand Rapids: Zondervan, 1990). See Introduction to Hebrews: Authorship.
2. Kenneth Barker, editor. *The NIV Study Bible* (Grand Rapids: Zondervan, 1985). See Introduction to Hebrews: Author.

These Hebrew Christians seem to have been hesitant about cutting themselves off decisively from the Jewish religion (which was tolerated by the Romans) in favor of the Christian way (which was not).[1] The early Christians suffered persecution, even death, at the hands of both Jewish and Roman authorities. As a result, the Hebrew Christians were being tempted to revert to Judaism or to add Jewish regulations to the gospel.

Theme

The theme of Hebrews, according to the *NIV Study Bible*, is the absolute supremacy and sufficiency of Jesus Christ as revealer and as mediator of God's grace.[2] The author develops this theme by showing the surpassing excellence of Christ over all that had gone before. The prophecies, practices and promises of the Old Testament (the Old Covenant) are fulfilled in the glory and reality of the Lord Jesus (the New Covenant).

You will note how frequently the word "better" or "superior" is used in Hebrews to show the excellence of what Christians possess. Among these is the assertion that Christ is "superior to the angels" (Hebrews 1:4), and that Christians have a "better hope" (Hebrews 7:19), "a better covenant" (Hebrews 7:22), "better promises" (Hebrews 8:6), and "better sacrifices" (Hebrews 9:23). There are also many "great" things mentioned—"a great salvation" (Hebrews 2:3), "a great high priest" (Hebrews 4:14), "the greater...tabernacle" (Hebrews 9:11), "a great contest in the face of suffering" (Hebrews 10:32), "a great reward" (Hebrews 10:35, NASB), "a great cloud of witnesses" (Hebrews 12:1), and the "great Shepherd of the sheep" (Hebrews 13:20).

Hebrews, written to encourage, speaks forcefully, yet with warmth and assurance. It shows that the things God has provided in Christ far surpass what came before in temple worship, for all the types (things that foreshadow something in the future) spoken of in the law are fulfilled in God's Son. This letter speaks to believers who had yielded to carelessness and backsliding, and who were in danger of throwing away their confidence in the finished work of Christ. Their weaknesses are contrasted with the person and work of Christ to show that to know Him is to demonstrate His power in consistent Christian living (see Philippians 4:13). The desire of our heavenly Father is that His Son may be "all in all" to those who profess His name (see 1 Corinthians 15:28; Ephesians 1:22-23), that they may know Him, learn more of Him, and be filled with the joy of a victorious moment-by-moment relationship with the risen Lord.

The letter to the Hebrews speaks today to all believers. Its message is profound yet practical. It urges believers to press on to maturity (see Hebrews 6:1). To plumb the depths of our treasure in the Lord Jesus Christ is an exciting, enriching experience. Hebrews makes known what Christ accomplished for you and me.

The Riches of God's Word

Looking beyond the particular difficulties the Hebrew believers encountered, we see another problem that also prevails today. Many who acknowledge Christ as Savior never progress beyond that point in Christian experience—they never mature in their faith and knowledge of Him. They are content with assurance of salvation; they move in Christian circles and practice religious habits. They are comfortable in their hope for the future, however vague that may be.

The secret of spiritual growth is reading, studying and applying God's Word, the Bible. Failure to read, study and apply God's Word leaves us with only the bare bones of Christian faith. Salvation through faith in the blood of Jesus Christ is a precious gift (see Ephesians 2:8-9), but it is only the beginning. God's plan is that we grow spiritually, learn the riches of His Word, and come to know Him in a more intimate relationship.

When we explore the Bible, we discover that teachings presented in its early pages recur and are expanded in its later portions. This unfolding of truth confirms the divine inspiration of the Bible. For example, the revelation of the coming Savior and God's plan of redemption may be traced from the first promise in Genesis 3:15 through the types in Leviticus and the foreshadowing in the Psalms and prophets. In the Gospel record, the prophecies of His birth, death and resurrection are fulfilled; and in Revelation the Lamb, the Lord Jesus Christ, is seen as the everlasting King of Kings and Lord of Lords.

Do you know the Lord Jesus as your personal Savior? That is the first step in knowing God and His Word. John 3:36 says, "Whoever believes in the Son has eternal life, but whoever rejects the Son will not see life, for God's wrath remains on him." And in Acts 4:12 Peter declared of Jesus Christ, "Salvation is found in no one else, for there is no other name under heaven given to men by which we must be saved."

Before you begin the study of Hebrews, will you receive the most precious gift of eternal life through faith in God's Son, the Lord Jesus Christ? This is a transaction between you and God. Jesus assures us, "I tell you the truth, whoever hears my word and believes him who sent me has eternal life and will not be condemned; he has crossed over from death to life" (John 5:24). Heaven is not achieved by doing great works or by any honor you may attain; it is a free gift of God. If you do not have a personal relationship with the Lord, why not make the decision now to put your trust in Him?

The privilege of every believer is to experience the fullness of Christ, His glory and His power. In your study of this letter to the Hebrews, may the Lord grant you "the Spirit of wisdom and revelation, so that you may know him better...[and] that the eyes of your heart may be enlightened" (Ephesians 1:17-18). May you accept its challenge to live in obedience to the Lord, that He might "equip you with everything good for doing his will, and...work in us what is pleasing to him, through Jesus Christ, to whom be glory for ever and ever" (Hebrews 13:21).

---

1. *The Expositor's Bible Commentary.* See Introduction to Hebrews: Destination.
2. *The NIV Study Bible.* See Introduction to Hebrews: Theme.

Study Questions

Before you begin your study this week:
- Pray and ask God to speak to you through His Holy Spirit.
- Use only the Bible for your answers.
- Write down your answers and the verses you used.
- Answer the "Challenge" questions if you have the time and want to do them.
- Share your answers to the "Personal" questions with the class only if you want to share them.

First Day: Read the Introduction to Hebrews.

1. What meaningful or new thought did you find in the Introduction to Hebrews or from your teacher's lecture? What personal application did you choose to apply to your life?

2. Look for a verse in the lesson to memorize this week. Write it down, carry it with you, or post it in a prominent place. Make a real effort to learn the verse and its "address" (reference of where it is found in the Bible).

Second Day: Read Hebrews 1:1-3, concentrating on verse 1.

1. How did God communicate with Old Testament believers, according to Hebrews 1:1?

2. Challenge: The writer of Hebrews begins with the reality of God and the fact that He has revealed Himself and His will many times and in many ways. Read and summarize the following examples of God's communication with His people in Old Testament times.

   Exodus 3:1-6

   1 Kings 19:9-13

   Isaiah 6:1-9

3. a. Read Exodus 33:18-20. Can a sinful human being look upon the face of God and live?

   b. Read Exodus 33:21-23. How did the Lord arrange for Moses to see Him and still live?

4. Personal: Although our sin prevents us from directly seeing God, He has throughout time reached out to His people, making a way to communicate with us. Can you see His love and concern for us demonstrated in these examples from the Old Testament? How does that make you want to respond to Him?

Third Day: Review Hebrews 1:1-3, concentrating on verse 2a.

1. a. In what time period has God's method of communication with mankind changed? (Hebrews 1:2a)

   b. How has He spoken to us in this time period? (Hebrews 1:2a)

2. Jesus is more than just the last one in a long line of prophets. His appearance begins a completely new time period, often called the "last days" in the Bible. What do you learn about the beginning of this time period in the following verses?

   Galatians 4:4-5

   Ephesians 1:9-10

3. Challenge: The God who spoke through the prophets is the same God that has spoken to us by his Son, Jesus Christ. The Old Testament communications prepared the way for the coming of Christ. What examples of this do you find in the following Scriptures?

   Isaiah 7:14 with Matthew 1:18-23

   Isaiah 53:4 with Matthew 8:16-17

4. Personal: Jesus was the very Son of God. He was divine in His essential nature, and yet He became fully human, in accordance with God's plan to speak to humankind through Him. Jesus knew the Old Testament Scriptures and what their fulfillment would mean for His earthly existence—suffering and death—yet He chose to obey His Father's will. What is your response to this? Write a prayer about this here.

Fourth Day: Review Hebrews 1:1-3, concentrating on verse 2b.

1. How does the writer of Hebrews begin to describe the Son, through whom God the Father has spoken to us? (Hebrews 1:2b)

2. First, Hebrews 1:2 says, God "appointed [His Son] heir of all things." In our everyday experience, a person becomes an "heir" only through the death of another. But in Scripture the term points to lawful possession without indicating in what way that possession is secured.[1] What do you learn in the following verses about Christ's lawful possession of and authority over all things?

   Matthew 28:18

---

1. *The Expositor's Bible Commentary.* See notes on Hebrews 1:2.

Philippians 2:9-11

3. Challenge: Read Romans 8:13-17. What amazing assertion does Paul make about our position if we are God's children through faith in Jesus Christ?

4. Hebrews 1:2 goes on to say that God made the universe "through" His Son. How do the following Scriptures confirm this?

    1 Corinthians 8:6

    Colossians 1:13,16

5. Personal: Think of it—God the Creator made our vast universe through His beloved Son, and gave Him lawful possession and complete authority over it. If we consider only this point, God and His Son seem so majestic and remote. How could any human being ever know God? Yet, Hebrews 1:2 says, God "*has spoken to us* by his Son." Have you heard God the Father's message of love and grace that He spoke through His Son, Jesus Christ? How have you responded?

Fifth Day: Review Hebrews 1:1-3, concentrating on verse 3a.

1. How else is the Son described in the first sentence of Hebrews 1:3?

2. In Jesus Christ we see the glory of God as it really is, yet He reveals His glory in a way that we can bear in our human weakness. (Remember what we read of Moses' experience with God's glory in Exodus 33:18-23 earlier this week.) How is this confirmed in the following verses?

    John 1:14

    2 Corinthians 4:6

3. The Son is also the "exact representation of [God's] being" (Hebrews 1:3). When we see Jesus, we see what God's real being is like. What do you learn about this in John 14:9?

4. The third descriptive phrase in Hebrews 1:3 tells us that Jesus is "sustaining all things." The Greek word translated "sustaining" means that Jesus is not only holding up the universe, but He is also carrying the universe along, bearing it toward a goal—the fulfillment of God's plan.[1] How does Colossians 1:17 express this?

5. Next we learn *how* Jesus is sustaining all things—"by his powerful word" (Hebrews 1:3). We may think of words as having no substance, but Jesus' word is active and it has force. Read the following verses for several examples.

    Matthew 8:16

---

1. Ibid. See notes on Hebrews 1:3.

Luke 4:38-39

Mark 4:37-41

6. Personal: Jesus shows us God's glory and who God really is. He is carrying along the whole universe in accordance with God's plan. Yet He cares deeply about every individual. While He was here on earth He used His powerful word to heal the sick and release people from evil powers. Do you believe that He cares about you, too—about every aspect of your life? Why not write a prayer here, expressing your confidence that He will sustain you?

Sixth Day: Review Hebrews 1:1-3, concentrating on verse 3b.

1. The writer of Hebrews now gets to the heart of the matter. What does he say the Son accomplished regarding sin? (Hebrews 1:3b)

2. The Son of God, Himself, came to deal decisively with the problem of our sin. The word purification indicates that sin defiles us—it stains us. How does Isaiah 64:6 describe our sinful nature?

3. Who provided purification for our sins, and how did He do this, according to 1 John 1:7?

4. What did the Son do after He provided purification for sins? (Hebrews 1:3b)

5. a. Challenge: Jesus Christ is now in the place of highest honor. Who put the Son in this place, according to the following verses?

    Philippians 2:9

    Ephesians 1:18-20

    b. Read Romans 8:34. What is Jesus doing from this place of honor?

6. Personal: Again we see Jesus' great love for us. Although He has accomplished His work of purification from sin and is seated in the place of highest honor at the right hand of His Father, He is not "taking it easy." Rather, He continually intercedes for us—pleads with the Father in support of us—that we might not suffer the due punishment for our sin. What does this mean to you?

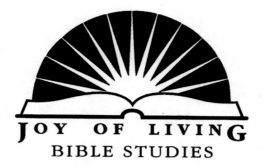

**Hebrews
Lesson 2**

JOY OF LIVING
BIBLE STUDIES

Hebrews 1:1-3

Hebrews 1:1-3 introduces the theme of the letter—the supremacy and sufficiency of Christ. The writer begins, "In the past God spoke to our forefathers through the prophets at many times and in various ways" (Hebrews 1:1). The Old Testament prophets of Israel were not merely wise men or visionaries, but people who spoke what was revealed to them by the Holy Spirit (see 1 Peter 1:10-12; 2 Peter 1:21). God employed various avenues of communication to convey revelations of Himself—visions, dreams, and even His audible voice.

Revelation in Scripture is progressive. God's entire purpose for the human race and the world about us was not given all at once. Little by little was God's way of communicating truths concerning Himself, His plan and purpose for Israel as a nation, and of extending to all people His salvation—that is, the forgiveness of sin and the presence of the Holy Spirit within the believer (see Romans 1:16; John 16:7-14). Like part of a jigsaw puzzle, no one truth was complete in itself.

For example, Genesis 3:15 refers to the coming Savior, and other Old Testament prophecies foretell His birth, death, and resurrection. Yet the fulfillment of God's plan was not recorded until hundreds of years later by New Testament writers, and the Savior's return to earth to reign as King of Kings is still in the future (see 1 Timothy 6:12-16).

The Covenants

When we view Scripture as a whole, we see how carefully and lovingly God has revealed Himself and His plan to us. The covenants, or promises, from God to His people progressively reveal His plan.

God alone established His covenants with humanity. He initiated each covenant, determined its elements, and confirmed it. People are the recipients of God's covenants, and our responsibility is to obey His commands.[1]

The Covenant at Creation

God's first covenant was established at Creation. Walter Elwell writes of this covenant, "[God] created his image-bearers by means of which he placed and kept man and woman in a close relationship with himself and had them mirror (reflect) and represent him within the created cosmos. Humanity was given stipulations or mandates. As im-

age-bearers they were to maintain an intimate and obedient fellowship with their Creator... God blessed Adam and Eve; he thus gave them ability and authority to serve as his covenant agents... He also spoke of the possibility of disobedience, if they ate of the forbidden tree of knowledge of good and evil (see Genesis 2:17). The ideas of blessing (life) and curse (death) thus were also included."[2]

The Covenant in Eden

Sadly, Adam and Eve believed the lies of Satan, disobeyed God, and thereby broke their covenantal relationship with Him. But God did not in turn break His covenant toward creation and humanity. Instead, He added another dimension to the creation covenant with the Edenic covenant, or the covenant of grace. This was His earliest promise of redemption. The sin and failure of Adam and Eve necessitated a Savior, promised first in Genesis 3:15. Fellowship was restored between God and humanity by God's assurance that the woman's offspring would be victorious over Satan and his offspring.

The Covenant to Noah

Next came the covenant God made to Noah following the Flood (see Genesis 9). God determined to wipe out sinful humankind, sparing only Noah and his family because of Noah's faith. After the Flood, Noah built an altar and sacrificed to God. God responded and confirmed His creation covenant to Noah, his descendants and every creature. Human government was instituted in order that sin might be held in check. Human life was to be protected, and murderers put to death. One of the prophecies in connection with the Noahic covenant indicates that Noah's son Shem would have a special place in God's plan. Shem was an ancestor of Abraham. (See Genesis 11:10-27.)

The Covenant to Abraham

God's covenant to Abraham promised, "I will make you into a great nation" (Genesis 12:2). This was fulfilled in the descendants of Jacob, to whom God gave the land of Israel for an everlasting possession. God promised that through Abraham all the peoples of the earth would be blessed (see Genesis 12:3), another revelation of the coming Savior. This covenant was marked by God's command that all Abraham's male offspring were to be circumcised. The promises were accompanied by commands, requiring both faith and obedience.

The Covenant at Mount Sinai

Further enlightenment concerning God's will and His commands is given in His covenant with Israel at Mount Sinai. God called Moses

---

1. Elwell, Walter A. "Entry for 'Covenant'". "Evangelical Dictionary of Theology". <http://bible.crosswalk.com/Dictionaries/BakersEvangelicalDictionary/bed.cgi>. 1997.

2. Ibid.

to be the covenant mediator. At Mount Sinai, God commanded Israel to obey His covenant. This obedience would keep Israel in covenantal relationship as God's chosen people.

God spoke the Ten Commandments in the hearing of the people, and then followed this with instruction to Moses explaining and applying these commandments to Israel's daily life. Sacrifices were offered to God, and the people were sprinkled with the blood of the covenant, sealing them as God's precious possession (see Exodus 24:8).

The Covenant to David

The climax of added revelation and expansion of God's covenant came when God addressed David through Nathan the prophet (see 2 Samuel 7:1-17).[1] God had chosen David, a humble shepherd, to be king over Israel. Now God promised, "Your throne shall be established for ever" (2 Samuel 7:16).

The future kingdom of Christ is founded in the Davidic covenant. According to Luke 3:23-28, Mary, the mother of the Lord Jesus, was a descendant of David's son, Nathan. (Although Luke identifies Joseph as "the son of Heli" in verse 23, the meaning appears to be "son-in-law." Heli was Mary's father, so this genealogy gives Mary's line.) The genealogy in Matthew 1:1-16 shows that Mary's husband descended from David's son Solomon, the royal line. It is through Joseph, "stepfather" of Jesus, that the throne legally passed to Christ.

The New Covenant

The new covenant, of which Jesus is mediator (see Hebrews 8:6-13), is established on the sacrifice of Christ. It is unconditional and irreversible, and secures eternal blessedness for every believer because of the completeness of our redemption in Christ Jesus and the glorious truth of the presence of the Holy Spirit within us. In sending His Son to personally represent Him, God accomplished the ultimate fulfillment of His plan.

So God's plan was outlined step by step through the covenants He has made. We are privileged to have access to all these truths, that we may view the panorama from eternity to eternity.

Christ's Superiority over the Prophets

The writer of Hebrews continues, "But in these last days [God] has spoken to us by his Son" (Hebrews 1:2a). In this statement he lays the foundation upon which all else rests—Jesus Christ, the eternal Word of God. God is the Source, Christ the channel through which endless blessings come into our lives, if we will only open ourselves to His forgiveness of our sin (see John 3:16-17) and to the empowerment of the Holy Spirit (see Romans 15:13; 1 Corinthians 2:4).

Consider the fact that God "has spoken" (Hebrews 1:2). Our God is not an impersonal, silent "first cause" or an unknowable deity. From the beginning of creation, He has spoken (see Genesis 1:3). He has issued promises, predictions, commands, and warnings. It wasn't enough that God spoke through angels and prophets; He ultimately chose to speak to us by His Son. We could never know deliverance

from sin or experience a relationship with God, except in the Son, the Word of God who "became flesh and made his dwelling among us" (John 1:14). It was not possible for Old Testament believers to know God as we may know Him today through saving faith in His Son.

When a person speaks, he indicates that he believes the one addressed is capable of understanding and exchanging thoughts and messages. That God has spoken is proof of His desire for fellowship with His children. He communicates His glory, His love, His blessings through His Word. People's words have influenced nations and changed the courses of history. Words carry weight, measured by what we think of the speaker, his wisdom, his knowledge of his subject, his truthfulness and forcefulness. What then should God's words be worth to us?

When a person speaks, he expects that those addressed will give him courteous attention. God asks that we listen as He speaks to us by His Son. Christ Himself is God's message to us. The Bible is the channel communicating His thoughts and purposes for our lives and for the world. But unless there is a response in our hearts, the fact that God has spoken will be of no effect in our lives. This truth is illustrated in the parable of the farmer recorded in Mark 4:1-20. Unless the "seed" of the Word is accepted—sprouting and producing a crop of faith—it will not be fruitful in our lives.

John 1:1-4, which speaks of Jesus, shows that God's Word is much more than a spoken Word: "In the beginning was the Word, and the Word was with God, and the Word was God. He was with God in the beginning. Through him all things were made; without him nothing was made that has been made. In him was life, and that life was the light of men." Jesus is the Living Word, evidenced in the lives of all who listen and yield to His presence and power.

The phrase, "In these last days" (Hebrews 1:2), refers to the entire period from the birth of Christ until His second coming to earth— so its message is for you and me. The glory of the Lord Jesus and His continued ministry as our high priest are explained in Hebrews. As we study this book, the words, "God has spoken," will become a reality and fill our hearts with joy and adoration. Have you heard Him say, "I tell you the truth, whoever hears my word and believes him who sent me has eternal life and will not be condemned; he has crossed over from death to life" (John 5:24)? Have you heard Him urging you to be filled with the knowledge of His will?

Spiritual wisdom and understanding will enable and empower you to live in a manner worthy of the Lord, to please Him in all things. Either you will hear God speaking in His Son, or you will turn an indifferent and deaf ear to His claims. How will you respond?

The Son Is Described

Hebrews 1:2b-3 continues by describing the Son: "whom he appointed heir of all things, and through whom he made the universe. The Son is the radiance of God's glory and the exact representation of his being, sustaining all things by his powerful word. After he had provided purification for sins, he sat down at the right hand of the Majesty in heaven."

---

1. "Entry for 'Covenant'". "Evangelical Dictionary of Theology".

The Son was much more than just another prophet through whom God spoke by the Holy Spirit. The verses before us show that Christ in His very nature transcended all that had been previously said or revealed. Seven propositions are outlined here which portray the glories of Jesus. They point up His qualifications as God's spokesman.

The first point is Christ's appointment as "heir of all things" (Hebrews 1:2). In our everyday experience, a son becomes an "heir" only through the death of the father. But in Scripture the term points to lawful possession without indicating in what way that possession is secured.[1] God has appointed Christ to be Possessor of the universe. (See Revelation 19:6-16; 22:1-21.)

Jesus confirmed His status as heir in Matthew 28:18, "All authority in heaven and on earth has been given to me." Evidence that He is heir will be realized when all nations are gathered before Him to be judged, and He exercises His right to separate the righteous from the unrighteous (see Matthew 25:31-46). But the greatest fulfillment of Christ's status as heir is seen in Revelation 22, where we read of the Holy City and the throne of God and of the Lamb. Honor and eternal power and authority belong to Him who is the "the blessed and only Ruler, the King of kings and Lord of lords" (1 Timothy 6:15).

What glory and riches God has given the One who chose to be humiliated for our sake. The Lord Jesus was poor when He lived on earth. He owned no home. His clothing was taken from Him at the cross; His burial place was borrowed. Every being, every angel, all the universe will acknowledge that He is Lord, for this is the reward God has given His Son, the Heir of all things (see Philippians 2:5-11).

The second point is that it was through the Son that God made the universe (see Hebrews 1:2). Christ is creator of time and space, and of all that is in the world as we know it. Colossians 1:16 affirms that all things have been created by Him and for Him. Everything was made according to His pattern, and He has put it all together in an order that surpasses human understanding. It is evident from Genesis 1:1-2, 26 that the three persons of the Trinity were active in creation.

The third point is, "The Son is the radiance of God's glory" (Hebrews 1:3). This expression means, "to send forth brightness or light," as sunbeams shining from the sun. The light we see is shining from the sun itself. We know the sun by its shining light. So Christ is the shining of the revelation of the glory of God (see John 1:14; 8:12; 12:35-36).

The fourth point is that the Son is "the exact representation of [God's] being" (Hebrews 1:3). The thought is of an engraving tool, a die or stamp used to give shape and detail to a coin or other object. The image pressed out by a mold or seal is the very same as the mold itself. None of the prophets of the Old Testament could come close to expressing God's nature. The Son perfectly expresses all that God is, for Christ is God. Jesus said, "Anyone who has seen me has seen the Father" (John 14:9).

The fifth point is that the Son is "sustaining all things by his powerful word" (Hebrews 1:3). The creator of all things also sustains all things. He governs and preserves that which He called into being. He keeps it all from becoming a jumbled mass of confusion. There is no such thing as the "law of nature." The universe was not created to run along without the direction and support of its Creator. All creation is directed by the will and word of its maker and sustainer. One word spoken by the Lord Jesus would dissolve His universe, so great is His power. The Lord Jesus revealed His power when He calmed the sea (see Mark 6:47-51), when He cast out demons (see Matthew 12:22-28), when He fed five thousand (see Mark 6:34-44) and when He brought Lazarus back from the dead (see John 11:1-45). These are only a few examples of His powerful word.

Far greater than the wonders of creation is the sixth point, that the Son "provided purification for sins" (Hebrews 1:3). The writer of Hebrews didn't hesitate to introduce the death of Christ as one of His highest glories, although the cross was a stumbling block to the Jews (see 1 Corinthians 1:23). More than God's spokesman, Christ is now seen as the great high priest who has made the matchless sacrifice for sin.

That Christ has put away our sins, paying for them with His blood, is the pinnacle of His work in the world. His work in making the universe and even in holding all things together is outshone by the wonders of His grace (unearned favor from God), and His exceeding mercy in redeeming sinners from Satan's grip. In His death on the cross, Christ fulfilled what was foreshadowed in the Old Testament sacrifices and offerings: Christ, God's perfect Lamb, died once for all. The apostle John wrote, "The blood of Jesus, his Son, purifies us from all sin" (1 John 1:7).

The seventh point is that the Son "sat down at the right hand of the Majesty in heaven" (Hebrews 1:3). When there's work to do, you cannot "sit down." This position of Christ at God's right hand speaks to us of His finished work. This is in contrast to Israel's priests who daily and continuously brought sacrifices. There was no chair in the tabernacle; their work was never finished. The "right hand" is a place of honor and authority.

The Son has fully accomplished God's purposes. Christ is God's Prophet, qualified to speak for Him. Christ is God's Priest, who has offered Himself as the sacrifice for sin. Christ is also God's King, and one day He will come again to bring to fulfillment His glorious kingdom (see Revelation 19-22).

The glories of our Lord Jesus Christ, His perfection, and the truths concerning Him should move our hearts not only to worship Him, but also to faithfully serve Him, by the power of the indwelling Holy Spirit (see Zechariah 4:6; 1 John 4:2,13).

Revelation 5:11-12 says, "Then I looked and heard the voice of many angels, numbering thousands upon thousands, and ten thousand times ten thousand. They encircled the throne and the living creatures and the elders. In a loud voice they sang: 'Worthy is the Lamb, who was slain, to receive power and wealth and wisdom and strength and honor and glory and praise!'" Can we not echo these words moment by moment, day by day?

---

1. *The Expositor's Bible Commentary.* See notes on Hebrews 1:2.

Study Questions

Before you begin your study this week:
- ❧ Pray and ask God to speak to you through His Holy Spirit.
- ❧ Use only the Bible for your answers.
- ❧ Write down your answers and the verses you used.
- ❧ Answer the "Challenge" questions if you have the time and want to do them.
- ❧ Share your answers to the "Personal" questions with the class only if you want to share them.

First Day: Read the Commentary on Hebrews 1:1-3.

1. What meaningful or new thought did you find in the commentary on Hebrews 1:1-3 or from your teacher's lecture? What personal application did you choose to apply to your life?

2. Look for a verse in the lesson to memorize this week. Write it down, carry it with you, or post it in a prominent place. Make a real effort to learn the verse and its "address" (reference of where it is found in the Bible).

Second Day: Read Hebrews 1:4-9, concentrating on verse 4.

1. How does the writer of Hebrews continue to describe the excellence of Christ in Hebrews 1:4?

2. Notice that Hebrews 1:4 begins with the word, "So...". What the writer asserts in verse 4 is based on what he just said in verse 3: It was because the Son "provided purification for sins," that He "sat down" in the place of highest honor, and it is in this aspect that Christ is seen as *becoming* superior to the angels.[1] As the fully divine Son of God, Christ is, of course, *eternally* superior to angels, who are created beings. What do you learn about this superiority in Colossians 1:15-18?

3. In Bible times, the name summed up all that a person was, and it made a statement about that person's character.[2] By what names is the Son identified in the following verses?

   Matthew 1:20-23

---

1. *The Expositor's Bible Commentary*. See notes on Hebrews 1:4.
2. Ibid.

Luke 1:30-32a

Revelation 19:11-13,16

4. How did the Son "inherit" His name, according to the following verses?

2 Peter 1:17

Philippians 2:9

5. When people realize their inferiority—how huge the gap is between themselves and God—they may be tempted to regard angels or other created beings as intermediaries between themselves and God. What does 1 Timothy 2:5-6 say about this?

6. Personal: Do you ever feel that you need someone to act as a go-between with God? Maybe you feel as if you have failed Him too many times, and you are not worthy to come directly to Him. The wonderful news from Hebrews is that we do have a mediator, Jesus Christ, who gave Himself for us. Have you allowed Him to mediate with God on your behalf, based on His payment on the cross for all your sin?

Third Day: Review Hebrews 1:4-9, concentrating on verse 5.

1. The writer of Hebrews now begins a series of quotations from the Old Testament, which all stress the superiority of Christ to the angels. What is the first quotation in Hebrews 1:5a? This passage quotes Psalm 2:7.

2. Although there is no explicit reference to the Messiah in Psalm 2:7, the writer of Hebrews considers this psalm to be a prophecy of the Messiah. Read Acts 13:32-33, which is part of a sermon Paul preached in a synagogue in Pisidian Antioch. How does Paul confirm this interpretation?

3. What is the second quotation from the Old Testament in Hebrews 1:5?

4. Hebrews 1:5b quotes 1 Chronicles 17:13, in which God is addressing David through Nathan the prophet. Though Nathan's words refer in the near future to David's son Solomon, what does 1 Chronicles 17:14 say that confirms Nathan's words are also a prophecy of the Messiah that would be a descendant of David?

5. Could any angel claim the relationship of "son" with God the Father? Read Revelation 22:8-9. How does the angel in this passage define the role of angels?

6. Personal: There is only one Son of God—Jesus Christ, yet many people continue to regard Him as merely a great teacher, or as a good example to follow. How do you regard Jesus Christ?

Fourth Day: Review Hebrews 1:4-9, concentrating on verse 6.

1. What additional support for Christ's superiority to angels does the writer of Hebrews give in Hebrews 1:6?

2. Jesus has the status with God that a firstborn son on earth has with his father.[1] What did Hebrews 1:2 say that illustrates this fact?

3. What else do you learn about Jesus' status as the firstborn in the following verses?

    Romans 8:29

    Colossians 1:15

    Colossians 1:18b

---

1. *The Expositor's Bible Commentary*. See notes on Hebrews 1:6.

4. Read Revelation 5:6-12. How do verses 11-12 fulfill God's command in Hebrews 1:6?

5. Personal: The One the angels worship—indeed, that all of heaven will worship—is clearly superior by far to them. Do you worship the Son, the Lord Jesus Christ? What does it mean to you to worship Him?

Fifth Day: Review Hebrews 1:4-9, concentrating on verses 7-8a.

1. What does the writer of Hebrews quote from the Old Testament about God's angels in Hebrews 1:7?

2. Note that Hebrews 1:8 begins with, "But..." How does the writer of Hebrews contrast the power of the Son in verse 8a with the power of the angels in verse 7?

3. Though God gives His angels the impressive power of wind and fire, yet they cannot measure up to the eternal, divine power of the Son. What do you learn about the eternal reign of the Son from Isaiah 9:6-7?

4. Personal: The power of wind and fire can be frightening and overwhelming to us. Think of wildfires that sweep through homes in a flash, or of hurricanes, tornados, cyclones and typhoons that devastate large areas. Do you fear and respect these powers? How much more do you fear and respect the power of the eternal Son of God?

Sixth Day: Review Hebrews 1:4-9, concentrating on verses 8b-9.

1. a. What will be the supreme characteristic of the kingdom of the Son, according to Hebrews 1:8b?

    b. Hebrews 1:8b continues the quotation of Psalm 45:6 from the Septuagint (see Day 4, Question 4). How does your English Bible translate Psalm 45:6 slightly differently?

2. What does the Son's concern for righteousness and justice lead God the Father to do? (Hebrews 1:9)

3. Challenge: Hebrews 1:9 says that God anointed the Son. Anointing was usually a rite of consecration to some sacred function. What are some examples of anointing from the following verses?

    Exodus 28:41 (God is speaking to Moses)

    1 Samuel 10:1

    1 Kings 19:16 (God is speaking to the prophet Elijah)

4. a. When God anointed the Son, He set the Son above His "companions." Read Hebrews 2:11 to see who these companions are.

    b. Hebrews 2:11 also tells us the sacred function for which the Son was anointed. What was it?

5. Hebrews 1:9 says that God anointed the Son "with the oil of joy." Read Isaiah 61:1-3, in which Isaiah speaks of the coming Messiah (see Luke 4:18-21, in which Jesus confirms that this passage refers to Himself). How does the Son give "the oil of joy" to all those who believe in Him?

6. Personal: Have you believed in the Son and received "the oil of joy" from Him? Write Isaiah 61:1-3, inserting your name to help you realize what the Son has given to you.

Hebrews Lesson 3

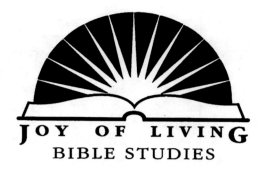

JOY OF LIVING
BIBLE STUDIES

Hebrews 1:4-9

The writer of Hebrews continues to describe the excellence of Christ—He is superior not only to the prophets, but to the angels. The word *angel* means messenger, and in Scripture it usually refers to a distinct order of created beings who are innumerable (see Hebrews 12:22). Angels possess intelligence, moral will, and emotions (see Psalm 103:20; Job 38:7). They are responsible before God to serve Him faithfully.

God's presence has been visibly manifested through angels who, at His direction, assume visible form. For example, when Abraham invited three strangers for dinner, he did not recognize that they were messengers from heaven until they told him of their errand (see Genesis 18-19). Later, the angel of the Lord stayed Abraham's hand from sacrificing his son, Isaac, when Abraham obeyed God's command (see Genesis 22). Angels urged Lot and his family to escape from Sodom, even taking hold of them to hurry their departure (see Genesis 19). God sent visible angels to reassure Jacob of God's presence with him (see Genesis 32:1-2). Angels were referred to as God's army at the battle of Jericho (see Joshua 5:13-15). And God sent angels to shut the lions' mouths and protect His faithful servant, Daniel (see Daniel 6).

Angels were present at the Creation (see Job 38:7). They appeared at the birth of the Savior, and ministered to Him after He endured Satan's temptation (see Luke 2:8-15; Matthew 4:1-11). In the garden of Gethsemane an angel appeared to Jesus and strengthened Him as He faced His upcoming arrest, trial and death (see Luke 22:43). Angels were present at Christ's resurrection and at His ascension, and will be with Him at His second coming (see Matthew 28:5-7; Acts 1:10; 2 Thessalonians 1:7).

The Bible identifies only two angels by name—Michael, the archangel (see Jude 1:9; Revelation 12:7-9); and Gabriel, who brought messages to Daniel (see Daniel 8:16-18; 9:21), announced the coming birth of John the Baptist (see Luke 1:18-19), and gave Mary the message about the conception of the Lord Jesus (see Luke 1: 26-31).

There are both good and bad angels. Fallen angels, also called demons, include Satan and those who followed him in his rebellion against God (see Isaiah 14:12-15; 2 Peter 2:4). Some of these fallen angels are bound in chains awaiting judgment (see Jude 6); others are yet unbound, acting as Satan's agents. Satan and his hosts promote hatred among men and opposition to God, and create havoc among families and nations. They are busy in the lives of individuals, seeking to discredit God and casting doubts on the Word of God. (See Job 1:6-12; Ephesians 6:16; 1 Peter 5:8.) Yet Satan will never be the victor in this battle! (See Revelation 20:10.)

Angels were highly regarded by the Jews at the time the letter to the Hebrews was written. Some people, conscious of their own inferiority, imagined a widening gap between themselves and God, and they began to think of angels as intermediaries between God and man, even going so far as to worship angels (see Colossians 2:18).

However, Scripture tells us that we may only approach the Father through His Son, who is the only mediator between God and man (see 1 Timothy 2:5-6). The writer of Hebrews shows that God's Son is far greater than angels, and that He is exalted to the right hand of the Father (see Hebrews 1:3), there to appear in the presence of God for us. Every Christian is privileged to come directly to God, because of what the Lord Jesus Christ has done for us.

That Worthy Name

Look again at how Hebrews 1:3 leads into verse 4, "After he had provided purification for sins, he sat down at the right hand of the Majesty in heaven. So he became as much superior to the angels as the name he has inherited is superior to theirs." It was because the Son "provided purification for sins," that He "sat down" in the place of highest honor, and it is in this aspect that Christ is seen as *becoming* superior to the angels.[1] As the fully divine Son of God, Christ is, of course, *eternally* superior to angels, who are created beings. He appears in God's presence, not to judge believers, but to make intercession for us.

The book of Hebrews contrasts the angels, who are servants, with the Son. Though the created angels are powerful and impressive, the Son's excellent name was obtained by inheritance, by His position as Son of God. Jesus, whose name is above every name (see Philippians 2:9), is declared to be "Wonderful Counselor, Mighty God, Eternal Father, Prince of Peace" (Isaiah 9:6).

"What's in a name?" we may ask. In our culture, we do not place much importance on names. In most cases, names for our children are not chosen for their meaning, and indeed some names seem to have no meaning at all. The Jews, however, attached great importance to

---

1. *The Expositor's Bible Commentary.* See notes on Hebrews 1:4.

names, which often had significant meanings. The name "LORD God" brings to mind many awesome and majestic revelations of God in the Old Testament. This name is the "I AM WHO I AM" of Exodus 3:14, unchanging and eternal. The Son is also "LORD God." It was His claim to this name that so angered the Jews, because they considered it blasphemy for anyone to dare to call himself by it. Matthew reports, "The high priest said to [Jesus], 'I charge you under oath by the living God: Tell us if you are the Christ, the Son of God.' 'Yes, it is as you say,' Jesus replied… Then the high priest tore his clothes and said, 'He has spoken blasphemy!'" (Matthew 26:63-65).

When the Lord Jesus was questioned concerning His statement, "Your father Abraham rejoiced at the thought of seeing my day; he saw it and was glad," He answered, "Before Abraham was born, *I am!*" (John 8:56,58, italics added). Had Jesus been less than the One He was, it would have been blasphemy to take the name that belonged only to God. Christ's declaration sets forth His preexistence, His priority and His person. Israel's rejection of Jesus was the rejection of the LORD God, for the Christ of the New Covenant is the LORD God of the Old Testament.

In John 18, when the group of men that came to arrest the Lord Jesus were asked, "Who is it you want?" they said, "Jesus of Nazareth." The Lord replied, "I am he," and at His words, they fell to the ground. Jesus, whom they came to take, was the LORD God; they could not stand before Him. His superior name is most surely the majestic, holy name LORD God. The Son is Immanuel, God with us (see Matthew 1:23).

Old Testament Confirmation

In Hebrews 1:5, the writer begins to quote a series of Old Testament passages to elaborate on the truth of Christ's superiority. He appeals to the authority of the Scriptures, acknowledged by every Jewish believer (see Psalm 19:7-8).

The Son of God

The first quotation comes from Psalm 2:7, "You are my Son; today I have become your Father." The writer of Hebrews clearly takes this psalm as a prophecy of the Messiah. The apostle Paul quotes the same passage in Acts 13:33, in speaking of the resurrection of Christ from the dead. Although in the Old Testament angels are sometimes called "sons of God" (see Job 1:6; 2:1; 38:7, NASB), the question, "For to which of the angels did God ever say…" explicitly excludes the multitude of heavenly hosts. God never addressed an angel as His Son.

The second quotation in Hebrews 1:5, "I will be his Father, and he will be my Son," comes from 2 Samuel 7:14. Although these words originally referred to David's son Solomon, the writer of Hebrews applies them to the Messiah, the ultimate descendant of David. These words are the expression of the eternal, unchangeable love of the Father for the Son, and the Son's unquestioning obedience and commitment to His Father.

The Firstborn

The word *firstborn* in Hebrews 1:6 is a title: Christ is the Firstborn, the expression of God's glory. This title reveals the love of the Father in sending the Son to redeem the lost (see John 3:16-17). When the Firstborn Son of God came into the world in Bethlehem, angels did not worship the infant Jesus; rather, they sang praises to the One who sent the Savior (see Luke 2:8-14). But when God again brings the Firstborn into the world at the Second Coming, then all the angels of God will worship Him (see Revelation 5:11-14). The redeemed, whose sin has been forgiven and who have received eternal life because of their faith in the Lord Jesus Christ, will join in adoration of the One who is altogether lovely (see Psalm 27:4).

The Son Is God

Hebrews 1:7 speaks of angels as winds and flames of fire. The symbolism depicts power, and swift and determined action in accomplishing their mission. Wind is one of the few things in creation that we cannot see. Like the wind, angels are invisible, and although we cannot see them, Scripture assures us that they minister to believers. God has given them great power, like strong winds. One instance is recorded in 2 Kings 19:35 where an angel swept through the Assyrian camp, putting to death 185,000 warriors. Fire speaks of the judgment of God, as seen in the angel's message to Lot concerning Sodom's destruction (see Genesis 19:12-24). Often when the Bible mentions the appearance of angels, they are accompanied by a shining light or great brilliance, as when Peter was released from prison by an angel (see Acts 12:7).

Though God gives His angels the impressive power of wind and fire, yet they cannot measure up to the eternal, divine power of the Son, who is King. The writer of Hebrews goes on to quote from Psalm 45:6-7, taking this psalm as a prophecy of the Messiah—"Your throne, O God, will last for ever and ever…" (Hebrews 1:8).

Scripture makes clear that angels are servants of God ministering to believers as God directs them. By contrast in Hebrews 1:8, the Son is addressed as "God" by the Father. This is positive proof of the deity of Christ. The Father Himself testifies that the Son is God; they are One. God declared that His Son's kingdom is eternal.

The Kingdom of Righteousness

Hebrews 1:8b (quoting Psalm 45:6) continues, "…and righteousness will be the scepter of your kingdom." A scepter is an emblem of authority. In the Old Testament Book of Esther, no one could appear before King Ahasuerus of Persia without a summons unless the king held out his golden scepter. Queen Esther risked her life when she approached the king unsummoned. When the king saw his lovely queen, he held out the scepter and Esther safely came near him (see Esther 4:10—5:3). God protected Esther and used her to deliver the Jews from Haman's wicked plot.

Even today, a royal monarch carries a scepter on state occasions as a symbol of power. A scepter does not have a crook like a shepherd's staff; it is a straight rod. So the government it represents should be upright and just, with equality for all. The scepter of Christ's kingdom is one of righteousness. His administration is impartial; His reign is perfect. Not all in authority today in governments around the world exemplify justice, truth and righteousness. But we know God still holds the world in His power, and His plan and purpose are even now being accomplished. One day Christ will return to earth and the final righteous judgment will take place.

The quote from Psalm 45 continues in Hebrews 1:9, "You have loved righteousness and hated wickedness; therefore God, your God, has set you above your companions by anointing you with the oil of joy." Christ Himself is righteous and holy. His earthly life demonstrated His love for righteousness and His abhorrence of evil. In testing and trial, He never sinned. On earth, Christ was a man of sorrows, knowing humiliation and living in the midst of evil (see Isaiah 53; 2 Corinthians 8:9; Philippians 2:6-8). But He was the Son who pleased His Father (see Matthew 3:17), and now God has anointed Him, honored Him and exalted Him, making Him both Lord and Christ (see Acts 2:36).

Christ came to put away sin; He brings righteousness and restoration to all who come to Him for forgiveness. Do you have assurance that your sins are buried in the deepest sea? (See Micah 7:9.) You may know this by trusting the Lord Jesus as your substitute for sin. His death on the cross was for you, and God has promised eternal life to all who come to Him. Your sins will be put away, never to be remembered against you (see Hebrews 10:15-17). This doesn't mean that your life will be perfect; but the Lord graciously invites the Christian to confess sin, and He is faithful to forgive and to cleanse us (see 1 John 1:9). Have you made Him Lord of your life? Have you put Him first in all things? Why not stop and pray about these things right now? God is graciously waiting to hear from each one of us. He is waiting and wanting to give us His love, His forgiveness, and His power to live each new day triumphantly in Christ. (See Ephesians 3:16; Galatians 5:5,16-18,22-25.)

Study Questions

Before you begin your study this week:

- ❧ Pray and ask God to speak to you through His Holy Spirit.
- ❧ Use only the Bible for your answers.
- ❧ Write down your answers and the verses you used.
- ❧ Answer the "Challenge" questions if you have the time and want to do them.
- ❧ Share your answers to the "Personal" questions with the class only if you want to share them.

First Day: Read the Commentary on Hebrews 1:4-9.

1. What meaningful or new thought did you find in the commentary on Hebrews 1:4-9 or from your teacher's lecture? What personal application did you choose to apply to your life?

2. Look for a verse in the lesson to memorize this week. Write it down, carry it with you, or post it in a prominent place. Make a real effort to learn the verse and its "address" (reference of where it is found in the Bible).

Second Day: Read Hebrews 1:10—2:4, concentrating on 1:10-12.

1. a. The writer of Hebrews continues his series of quotations from the Old Testament, which all stress the superiority of Christ. Look back to Hebrews 1:5-6 to see who is speaking in Hebrews 1:10, "He also says…"

   b. What does God say about His Son in Hebrews 1:10-12? This passage quotes Psalm 102:25-27.

2. In the Old Testament these words were applied to God the Father, for His Son had not yet been revealed. Read John 1:1-3,14. What do you learn about the Son's work at Creation?

3. a. What does Hebrews 1:11 say will happen to the universe that we know today?

   b. How will the Son eventually deal with the creation that is wearing out? (Hebrews 1:12a)

4. a. Our universe is not as permanent as it seems. What do you learn in 2 Peter 3:10 about its fate?

    b. From 2 Peter 3:13, what will the Son replace the old created "garment" with after rolling up the old one?

5. a. Who remains the same, even as the creation is wearing out? (Hebrews 1:12b)

    b. How does Hebrews 13:8 confirm this?

6. Personal: How do you feel when you think about the fate of the created universe? Have you put your faith and trust in the One who created it and who will always be the same? Read Revelation 3:20. This same Creator and sustainer of the universe wants to come in and fellowship with you, if you will only open the door of your heart to Him.

Third Day: Review Hebrews 1:10—2:4, concentrating on 1:13.

1. a. In Hebrews 1:13, what question does the writer of Hebrews ask to introduce the final Old Testament quotation stressing the superiority of Christ? (Hebrews 1:13a)

    b. What answer do you think he expects to this question?

2. What does God say to His Son in Hebrews 1:13b? This is a quotation from Psalm 110:1.

3. Read Luke 1:19 and Revelation 8:2. What position do angels assume in the presence of God? How does this confirm that God would not say, "Sit at my right hand" (Hebrews 1:13) to an angel?

4. a. It is a mark of superiority that Christ sits at God's right hand. What does Hebrews 1:13b say God will do for His Son as He sits in this place of honor?

b. How has God done this, according to Colossians 2:15?

5. How does Ephesians 1:19b-23 confirm Christ's position and God the Father's action on behalf of His Son?

6. Personal: God says He will render all Christ's enemies completely powerless. Does the power of evil in the world today ever cause you to fear or despair? God's promise to His Son has *already* been fulfilled. We don't yet see with our eyes the defeat of evil, but we can trust God that Christ has triumphed over all. If you struggle with fear, why not talk to God about this now?

Fourth Day: Review Hebrews 1:10—2:4, concentrating on 1:14.

1. The writer of Hebrews now contrasts the angels with the Son. In comparison to Christ's royal position, what is the position of all angels? (Hebrews 1:14)

2. Who else, beside the Lord, do all angels serve? (Hebrews 1:14)

3. Challenge: The Book of Acts lists many instances when angels rendered service to believers. In each passage, what did angels do and for what purpose?

    Acts 5:17-20

    Acts 10:1-5,33

    Acts 12:5-11

Acts 27:21-25

4. Personal: God still cares for His people today, just as He did for the early Church. We may not often experience the individual visit of an angel today, but that doesn't mean angels are not continuing to serve believers as God commands. Do you trust in God's care for you, whether through the ministry of His Holy Spirit within you or through the service of His angels? Have you thanked Him for this care and service? Why not write a prayer of thanks here?

Fifth Day: Review Hebrews 1:10—2:4, concentrating on 2:1-3a.

1. a. Since—as the writer of Hebrews has demonstrated in chapter 1—the Son is so much superior to the angels, what must we do? (Hebrews 2:1a)

   b. The word translated "pay more careful attention" means not only to turn the mind to a thing, but also to act upon what one perceives.[1] What will happen if we do not do this? (Hebrews 2:1b)

2. Challenge: In Hebrews 2:2, the "message spoken by angels" refers to the Law of Moses.[2] Although the Old Testament does not speak of angels in connection with the giving of the Law, how do the following New Testament passages affirm this viewpoint?

   Acts 7:52-53

   Galatians 3:19

3. What authority did the Law have over those who received it, and what was the consequence for breaking it? (Hebrews 2:2)

4. How does the argument in Hebrews 2:2-3a demonstrate the superiority of the message that came through Christ over the message spoken by angels (the Law)?

---

1. *The Expositor's Bible Commentary*
2. Ibid.

5. Personal: Notice that the disaster that a person faces without the salvation offered through Jesus Christ is brought on, not by great and terrible sins, but by mere neglect, by ignoring His salvation. Have you actively responded to Jesus' message of salvation, and received His free gift of forgiveness of all your sin?

Sixth Day: Review Hebrews 1:10—2:4, concentrating on 2:3b-4.

1. Who first announced this great salvation? (Hebrews 2:3b)

2. Read Luke 19:1-10. How did Jesus announce this salvation in verses 9-10?

3. a. Who confirmed this salvation? (Hebrews 2:3b)

    b. How does Luke 1:1-2 describe these people who confirmed the message of salvation through Jesus Christ?

4. Who also confirmed this salvation, and in what way? (Hebrews 2:4)

5. In the following verses, how did the apostle Paul say that God confirmed his proclamation of salvation through Jesus Christ?

    Romans 15:18-19a

    2 Corinthians 12:12

6. Personal: Jesus announced and accomplished our great salvation. The apostles confirmed and preached this salvation, and God the Father testified to their message by signs and miracles through the Holy Spirit. We are privileged to have a written record of all these things in Scripture, God's Word to us. As you study God's Word, you are preparing yourself to share the message of this great salvation with others around you, just as the apostles did. Whom is God laying on your heart to share with this week?

Hebrews
Lesson 4

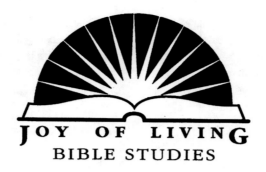

JOY OF LIVING
BIBLE STUDIES

Hebrews 1:10—2:4

Over the years I have enjoyed being present at a number of "beginnings." One was the first campaign meeting of America's best-known evangelist. Another was a midnight ride on the first train to travel over the Chicago subway system. Then there was the excitement of turning the first shovel full of dirt for the new campus of a Christian university. Beginnings are special. When they are related to the Lord's work, it is a joy to see how God guides and blesses as time marches on.

Christ the Creator

In Hebrews 1:10, God says of His Son, "In the beginning, O Lord, you laid the foundations of the earth, and the heavens are the work of your hands." Have you ever pondered the words "in the beginning"? Before time was, Christ laid the foundations of the earth, not using pre-existent material, but calling forth the earth and heavens by the Word of His power. His oneness with God is affirmed as He is declared to be the Creator, not only of the earth, but also of the heavens. The truth of the existence "in the beginning" of God the Father, Son and Holy Spirit boggles the finite mind.

The world has passed through many changes. All around us are symptoms of a dying world. We used to take for granted that its resources would last forever. Now we face shortages of fuel, food, and water. Pollution fills the air we breathe. Sin has marred the work of the Creator. Much of the natural beauty of the earth has been destroyed by developers who literally move mountains. The world about us is like a worn-out garment (see Hebrews 1:11), devastated by the ever-increasing masses of humanity. That the Lord will "roll them up like a robe" (Hebrews 1:12) is no less a demonstration of infinite power than the wonder of Job's declaration that He "suspends the earth over nothing" (Job 26:7).

The earth and the heavens will perish, but Christ will remain. Though all else may change or disappear, He is the same. Christ our Redeemer is not only almighty and sovereign, but also eternal: "But you remain the same, and your years will never end" (Hebrews 1:12). This Mighty One, the Sustainer of the universe, is the One who indwells believers to uphold, to strengthen, to empower those whose life is hidden with Christ in God (see Colossians 3:3).

Christ Triumphant

You have observed that, beginning at Hebrews 1:5, the author has quoted from the Psalms and from 2 Samuel to teach the superiority of Christ over angels. Christ's authority above angels is again emphasized in the quotation from Psalm 110:1: "To which of the angels did God ever say, 'Sit at my right hand until I make your enemies a footstool for your feet'?" (Hebrews 1:13). The Lord Jesus, the Son of God, is seated because His work is completed. In giving Himself as a sacrifice for your sin and mine, He fulfilled every obligation of the Law.

One would not suppose that such a glorious Savior would have enemies, yet many have aligned themselves with Satan, the arch-enemy. Sin is Christ's enemy, and so are death and the grave. Nations are His enemies in refusing His authority and sovereignty. The figure of speech, "a footstool for your feet" (Hebrews 1:13) reminds us of the symbol of victory in Joshua 10:24, where the captains of Israel's army put their feet on the necks of the conquered enemy kings. In Christ's ultimate triumph, all His enemies will be made His footstool; every knee will bow and every tongue confess Him, either in humble submission, or in subjection (see Romans 14:11).

Ministering Spirits

While angels are not given a place at God's right hand, they do have an important and unique position. They are "ministering spirits sent to serve those who will inherit salvation" (Hebrews 1:14). The angels' sphere of ministry involves physical protection and preservation, although their forms are not visible to us. Angels are superior to humans, yet are their servants, guarding and protecting believers. At God's direction, angels also execute judgment on His enemies.

Scripture contains many instances of angels protecting God's people. When the king of Syria sought to kill Elisha the prophet, he sent his army by night to the city of Dothan. Upon arising next morning, Elisha's servant ran fearfully to his master with the news that the king's army and chariots were circling the city. "'Don't be afraid,' the prophet answered. 'Those who are with us are more than those who are with them'" (2 Kings 6:16). Then Elisha prayed that the Lord would open the eyes of the servant, that he too might see the wonders of his God. "Then the Lord opened the servant's eyes, and he looked and saw the hills full of horses and chariots of fire all round Elisha" (2 Kings 6:17).

When Corrie Ten Boom and her sister, Betsie, were taken to the Nazi prison camp, Ravensbruck, they hoped they could keep their warm woolen undergarments and their Bible. However, all prisoners were searched and deprived of all possessions. Corrie and her sister asked permission to use the restroom. This gave them opportunity to remove their underwear, and to leave it and the Bible in a corner. Later, after showering and receiving prison clothing, Corrie retrieved the articles and hid them under her dress. The bulge was obvious, so she prayed that angels would surround her and that the guards would not see her. Although the woman ahead of her and the one following were thoroughly searched, Corrie was passed over, not by one guard only, but by two. God used Corrie in that prison camp to share His Word, giving assurance of God's love, of peace through the blood of the cross and of the joy of eternal life.

The Bible reminds us that angels may be fully visible, appearing as persons yet not recognized. Abraham entertained three strangers, later realizing that they were angels sent with a message from the Lord (see Genesis 18; Hebrews 13:2).

Billy Graham told the story of a group of American Marines during the Korean War who were trapped in subzero weather without food. They considered surrender their only chance for survival until a Christian in their group pointed out verses of Scripture that gave hope and encouragement. He taught them to sing a song of praise to the Lord. Miraculously a wild boar charged into their midst and dropped dead, providing food and strength for the starving men. Next morning they heard what they suspected was a Chinese patrol approaching, but their fears were unfounded. A South Korean soldier appeared. He spoke English, telling them to follow him. He led them through the forest to safety behind their own lines. As they began to thank him, he suddenly vanished.

Do you feel trapped by circumstances, discouraged by difficulties that seem insurmountable? Take courage! Satan's attacks are aimed at the Lord's faithful followers. Satan is not concerned with wicked people; he knows they are his servants. God's ministers, His angels, are guarding you (see Psalm 34:7). Remember that Satan cannot pierce the hedge that God has put around you. Fully put your trust in God's help and deliverance.

Attention Please!

When you hear the words "Attention please" in an airport or railroad terminal, you "tune in" to hear if the announcement gives direction for your journey. Not listening could cause delay, embarrassment, or possibly the cancellation of your trip. This letter warns Hebrew Christians against falling back into Judaism. It also warns against a superficial profession of faith in Christ, urging believers to go on to spiritual maturity, giving the Savior His place as Lord of our lives.

The author puts it this way: "We must pay more careful attention, therefore, to what we have heard, so that we do not drift away" (Hebrews 2:1). The word *therefore* is a pivot; on it attention is turned from all that was said in chapter 1 about God's Son—His excellence, His position and His authority—to the warning that follows in chapter 2.

The Hebrew Christians had read the Old Testament and had heard the gospel. Here they are urged to give careful consideration to what they know to be God's Word, to yield in obedience to its commands, to apply it to their lives. Failure to pay attention to what God reveals to us in His Word may result in drifting away from it.

The story is told of a yacht on a pleasure trip down the Niagara River. Its occupants went ashore for an hour or so, and upon returning to the dock found the ship had slipped her moorings. The owner and his friends were dismayed to discover the vessel had drifted to the brink of the falls and was lodged against the rocks. A crewman confessed that in his haste to join his friend ashore, he had neglected to tie up the ship securely. The beautiful yacht was soon battered and broken by the raging current. The world constantly tugs at the believer as Satan shows you its glitter and glamour. Or he just makes sure your life is cluttered with things that take your time and pull you away from the study of God's Word. You soon find yourself drifting dangerously close to total neglect of spiritual things.

The Law Is Binding

Hebrews 2:2-3a warns, "For if the message spoken by angels was binding, and every violation and disobedience received its just punishment, how shall we escape if we ignore such a great salvation?" The Hebrew Christians knew it was important to pay close attention to Moses and the prophets, "the message spoken by angels." The giving of the law at Sinai was an occasion of great importance to every Israelite. There is no definite mention of the presence of angels at Sinai, but there is an allusion to it in Deuteronomy 33:2, "The LORD came from Sinai and dawned over them from Seir; he shone forth from Mount Paran. He came with myriads of holy ones from the south, from his mountain slopes." New Testament authors also confirm the presence of angels at the giving of the Law (see Acts 7:52-53; Galatians 3:19).

The author points out that those to whom the Law was given found it valid. Its truth had been proven by experience. When they obeyed they enjoyed God's blessing; when they disobeyed they were punished. No more graphic illustration of this pattern is found in the history of any other people; for when Israel defied God's law, death followed. Numbers 15:30 warns, "But anyone who sins defiantly, whether native-born or alien, blasphemes the LORD, and that person must be cut off from his people." Other penalties, though less stringent, were designated for every breach of God's law. Time and again, Israel was reminded to pay attention to the things God taught them (see Deuteronomy 4:9; Isaiah 48:18).

So Great a Salvation

Moses was the first to instruct Israel to listen carefully to the One God would raise up to bring salvation: "The LORD your God will raise up for you a prophet like me from among your own brothers. You must listen to him" (Deuteronomy 18:15; see also John 1:45). God the Father proclaimed of Jesus, "This is my Son, whom I have chosen; listen to him" (Luke 9:35). Jesus Himself said, "For God so loved the world that he gave his one and only Son, that whoever believes in him shall not perish but have eternal life" (John 3:16). Neglect of the remedy that Jesus provided for sin brings death. If you have never received Christ as your Savior, will you make that decision now, and be assured of eternal life through faith in Christ's redeeming blood? What must you do to be lost?—Nothing.

The author of Hebrews continues, "This salvation, which was first announced by the Lord, was confirmed to us by those who heard him. God also testified to it by signs, wonders and various miracles, and gifts of the Holy Spirit distributed according to his will" (Hebrews 2:3b-4). The power of the gospel was confirmed in those who believed and whose lives were changed. It was further demonstrated in the wonder-working power of the Holy Spirit. The greatest sign was the resurrection of Jesus Christ. There were also healings by the apostles. A number of miracles are recorded in Acts, such as the raising of Tabitha from the dead (see Acts 9:40).

Acts 4 records the arrest of Peter and John and their appearance before the rulers and elders of Jerusalem. Those who questioned them were astonished at Peter's concise and convincing reply to their questions. He pointed to the man who had been healed as proof of the power of the resurrected Christ. His confidence in declaring, "Salvation is found in no one else, for there is no other name under heaven given to men by which we must be saved" (Acts 4:12), silenced the council. Their conclusion? They marveled and recognized Peter and John as having been with Jesus. This is what the good news is all about. It is the power of God to change lives. The indwelling Holy Spirit will empower and enable you to effectively witness for Him and to live according to His will.

Study Questions

Before you begin your study this week:

- ❧ Pray and ask God to speak to you through His Holy Spirit.
- ❧ Use only the Bible for your answers.
- ❧ Write down your answers and the verses you used.
- ❧ Answer the "Challenge" questions if you have the time and want to do them.
- ❧ Share your answers to the "Personal" questions with the class only if you want to share them.

First Day: Read the Commentary on Hebrews 1:10—2:4.

1. What meaningful or new thought did you find in the commentary on Hebrews 1:10—2:4 or from your teacher's lecture? What personal application did you choose to apply to your life?

2. Look for a verse in the lesson to memorize this week. Write it down, carry it with you, or post it in a prominent place. Make a real effort to learn the verse and its "address" (reference of where it is found in the Bible).

Second Day: Read Hebrews 2:5-18, concentrating on verses 5-8.

1. Look back at Hebrews 1:13. How does this help you understand Hebrews 2:5?

2. How does Hebrews 2:6-8a compare to Psalm 8:4-6?

3. a. Put the psalmist's question (from Hebrews 2:6b; Psalms 8:4) in your own words.

   b. How does the psalmist show that God has given man significance? (Hebrews 2:7-8a; Psalms 8:5-6)

4. God has made man supreme among the beings of this created world. But what does Hebrews 2:8b say is the current reality that we see around us?

5. Challenge: The full promise of Psalm 8 will not be fulfilled until Christ returns. In the meantime, we live in a world in which we struggle with limitations and frustrations. How does Romans 8:19-23 express this?

6. Personal: Do you experience frustration and limitation in your daily life? How do you react? Have you learned to turn to God and allow Him to work in and through you, even in the midst of these things? (See Romans 8:28-29.)

Third Day: Review Hebrews 2:5-18, concentrating on verse 9.

1. Although we do not yet see the fulfillment of Psalms 8:4-6 in mankind at large (see Second Day, question 2), in whom does the author of Hebrews say that it is already fulfilled? (Hebrews 2:9a)

2. a. What phrase in Hebrews 2:9 shows that Jesus was truly incarnate and has gone through the experience of living out this earthly life?

   b. How does Paul describe this in Philippians 2:5-7?

3. a. According to Hebrews 2:9, why was Christ crowned with glory and honor?

   b. How does Philippians 2:8-11 express this?

4. a. For what purpose did Jesus die, according to Hebrews 2:9?

   b. What do you learn about this in the following verses?

      2 Corinthians 5:14-15

      1 John 2:2

5. Personal: By God's grace Jesus died for us. It is also by God's grace that we can accept His sacrifice on our behalf, and be saved by faith in Him. Have you accepted this gift of faith leading to salvation? If so, whom do you need to tell about this precious gift?

Fourth Day: Review Hebrews 2:5-18, concentrating on verses 10-13.

1. As God carried out His eternal purpose to provide salvation for sinful man, what did He do with Jesus Christ according to the author of Hebrews? (Hebrews 2:10)

2. It is surprising to read that Jesus was "made perfect through suffering." The Expositors Bible Commentary notes, "There is a perfection that results from actually having suffered and that this is different from the perfection of being ready to suffer. The bud may be perfect, but there is a difference between its perfection and that of the flower."[1] Read Hebrews 4:15. Did Jesus ever sin?

3. a. What does Jesus call those who have been made holy through faith in Him? (Hebrews 2:11)

   b. What do you learn about this in the following verses?

      Matthew 12:49-50

      Romans 8:29

4. a. What does the author of Hebrews quote from Psalm 22:22 in Hebrews 2:12 that confirms the spiritual brotherhood of Jesus with those He saves?

   b. It was natural for the author of Hebrews to see Jesus as the speaker in Psalm 22, which is a messianic psalm that was fulfilled in Him. Many of its verses describe His experience on the cross. What did Jesus quote from this psalm as He hung on the cross? (Mark 15:34; Psalm 22:1a)

5. a. What does the author next quote in Hebrews 2:13 from Isaiah 8:17b-18a? Here we see that the Father's children are given to the Son to be His brothers.[2]

   b. Challenge: Read John 17:1-6. What do you learn about the fact that God has "given" all believers to Jesus Christ?

---

1. *The Expositor's Bible Commentary*
2. *The NIV Study Bible*.

6. Personal: If you are a believer, have you realized that you are not only a child of God, but also a brother or sister of Jesus Christ? What a privilege! Think of how you might look up to and follow the example of an older sibling in your earthly family. Do you also want to be like your spiritual older brother, Jesus Christ?

Fifth Day: Review Hebrews 2:5-18, concentrating on verses 14-15.

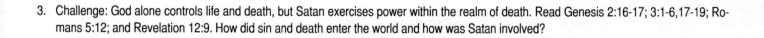

1. What nature does Jesus share with us? (Hebrews 2:14a)

2. Since Jesus shares this nature, what did His death accomplish? (Hebrews 2:14b)

3. Challenge: God alone controls life and death, but Satan exercises power within the realm of death. Read Genesis 2:16-17; 3:1-6,17-19; Romans 5:12; and Revelation 12:9. How did sin and death enter the world and how was Satan involved?

4. What does Christ's destruction of Satan do for all who trust in Him? (Hebrews 2:15)

5. Read Revelation 1:18. What does Jesus declare here that confirms His ability to do this?

6. Personal: Are you burdened with the hopeless and enslaving fear of death? Write John 3:16, inserting your name in place of "the world" and "whoever." Do you believe in the power of Jesus Christ to release you from slavery to the fear of death? Why not pray about this now?

Sixth Day: Review Hebrews 2:5-18, concentrating on verses 16-18.

1. What order of created beings did Jesus come to rescue, and with what group within that order was He identified in the Incarnation? (Hebrews 2:16)

2. What was the specific purpose of the Incarnation? (Hebrews 2:17)

3. Challenge: This is the first time in the book of Hebrews that the author calls Jesus a "high priest" who makes atonement for sin. Jesus' saving work fulfilled all the ceremonies of the Old Testament's Day of Atonement. What do you learn about this ceremony in Leviticus 16:29-34?

4. Why is Jesus able to help us when we are being tempted? (Hebrews 2:18)

5. How did Jesus suffer when He was tempted in the following Scriptures? Summarize briefly.

    Matthew 4:1-11

    Matthew 26:36-46

6. Personal: We know that Jesus was perfect and did not sin, so it's easy to think that He was above all the temptations and suffering that we experience in our weakness. But He lived as a real man, who experienced real temptation and real suffering. He knows what you are going through, no matter how terrible it is. He is waiting with compassion and love to help you. What are you facing that you need help with? Why not pray about it now?

Hebrews
Lesson 5

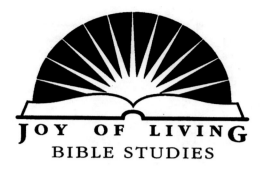

JOY OF LIVING
BIBLE STUDIES

Hebrews 2:5-18

Hebrews 2:5 declares, "It is not to angels that he has subjected the world to come, about which we are speaking." Important though angels are in God's universe, they will not be given rulership over the "world to come." Instead, as we will see, the heirs of salvation—those who have faith in Jesus Christ—will reign with Him (see 2 Timothy 2:12). The writer was encouraging Hebrew Christians to "hang in there" in anticipation of the glory that would be theirs. Angels could never sing redemption's song, nor would they share in the inheritance of Christ's blood-bought heirs of salvation (see Revelation 19:5-9; 21:1-7).

Hebrews 2:6-8a continues, "But there is a place where someone has testified: 'What is man that you are mindful of him, the son of man that you care for him? You made him a little lower than the angels; you crowned him with glory and honor and put everything under his feet.'" The writer quotes these verses from Psalm 8, which speaks of God's creation of mankind in a position of authority over the earth and its creatures. Mankind is placed in God's order of creation only a short way below the angels, setting him above all else in creation.[1]

Psalm 8 itself begins, "O LORD, our Lord, how majestic is your name in all the earth! You have set your glory above the heavens... When I consider your heavens, the work of your fingers, the moon and the stars, which you have set in place..." (Psalm 8:1-3). David may have written these words as he shepherded his flock on the hills of Bethlehem. Enjoying the majestic wonders of God's creation caused him to consider the work of God's fingers. God's glory and power shine through the beauty of the sun, the moon and the stars. God's creation is not only for man's admiration, but also for man's benefit. The psalmist marveled that the all-powerful, infinite God, the Creator and Sustainer of the universe, takes thought of insignificant man. He asks, "What is man that you are mindful of him?" (Psalm 8:4; Hebrews 2:6).

David makes an amazing observation about man: "You crowned him with glory and honor and put everything under his feet" (Hebrews 2:7-8a; from Psalm 8:5-6). Have you noticed that the verbs are past tense? When God speaks, it is as though it were already done; His Word is final, His promises sure.

In case anyone should question man's present position, the writer explains that we do not yet see the fulfillment of God's purposes. Hebrews 2:8b says, "Yet at present we do not see everything subject to

1. *The Expositor's Bible Commentary*

him." God created man and woman in His own image, to have the mastery over all creation (see Genesis 1:26-31), but disobedience changed their status. The sin of Adam and Eve resulted in consequences that affected the entire human race. God told Adam that creation would no longer work for him, but in opposition to him: "Cursed is the ground because of you; through painful toil you will eat of it all the days of your life. It will produce thorns and thistles for you, and you will eat the plants of the field. By the sweat of your brow you will eat your food until you return to the ground, since from it you were taken; for dust you are and to dust you will return" (Genesis 3:17-19). The sentence of death because of sin was passed down from Adam to all mankind.

Although we do not yet see the fulfillment of Psalms 8:4-6 in mankind at large, the writer of Hebrews goes on to declare in whom it is already fulfilled: "But we see Jesus, who was made a little lower than the angels, now crowned with glory and honor because he suffered death, so that by the grace of God he might taste death for everyone" (Hebrews 2:9). The Lord Jesus Christ gave up heaven's glory, became man and suffered the indignities and humiliation of death on the cross to redeem us from our fallen state. Now Christ has been exalted and restored to the place of honor He has had from the beginning with the Father (see John 17:5).

Hebrews is telling us that humanity's position is not currently the one of authority that God instituted, but this is only temporary. God will exalt His people to the first place among creatures. Look at Jesus. His suffering and death were humiliating, yet God has crowned Him with glory and honor. No longer does the Savior wear the crown of thorns. This is the pledge that God will do as He has promised for those who are the heirs of salvation.

Hebrews 2:9 says that Jesus "suffered death, so that by the grace of God he might taste death for everyone." It was by God's grace that Christ's saving work was accomplished. God in His great love and mercy permitted His Son to die. Christ "tasted death" for every man, woman and child who will accept Him as his or her Substitute. God was not required to be merciful to rebellious sinners. Man could not claim nor earn favors from Him. It was all a part of God's working all things in conformity with the purpose of His will (see Ephesians 1:11). It is solely the sovereign grace of God that makes salvation available to all men (see Titus 2:11).

Before raising Lazarus from the dead, Jesus said to Martha, "Whoever lives and believes in me will never die. Do you believe this?"

(John 11:26). Her response was, "Yes, Lord...I believe that you are the Christ, the Son of God, who was to come into the world" (John 11:27). Have you responded in faith to the Lord Jesus, as Martha did? The choice is up to you alone.

Follow Your Leader, Jesus Christ

Hebrews 2:10 continues, "In bringing many sons to glory, it was fitting that God, for whom and through whom everything exists, should make the author of their salvation perfect through suffering." The word translated "author" in the NIV may also be translated "captain" (NKJV), "leader" (NLT) or "pioneer" (RSV). In times past, it was customary for the captain of a regiment to lead his soldiers, encouraging and inspiring them. Nowadays officers usually stay behind the lines issuing orders. The Captain of our salvation, Jesus Christ, goes before us, leading, commanding, and encouraging. He is our guide and will see us safely through. He is all-powerful and faithful, and He is the guarantor of our victory. All the work of our glorious salvation is in His hands (see Luke 1:68,77).

Do you fully trust the Author or Leader of your salvation? His followers must be faithful, available and teachable. They will know God's blessings because they are willing to commit themselves totally to Christ. The Lord Himself was made perfect in meekness and submission so that He might bring you along that same path to enjoy all the glory to come. Our Leader is not only an example and influence—He is God, who in the person of the Holy Spirit dwells within us (see John 14:16-17). He is our life.

Why Am I Here?

The author of Hebrews describes God as "for whom and through whom everything exists" (Hebrews 2:10). All creation exists for one reason only: to show the glory of God. The goodness of the Lord shines out in all nature, in every towering mountain, in the tranquil lake or turbulent stream. If you've seen the beauty of a sunrise or a sunset, you have enjoyed the loveliness of the Savior. Such a sight causes the heart to sing, "May Jesus Christ be praised!" Yet these superb glories fade into insignificance when we think of God's purpose for Christians, who are the heirs of salvation. God has made us for His glory, so that we might share in the riches of His grace (see Ephesians 2:6-7). He has a plan for you and has promised to perfect His work in you and through you (see Philippians 1:6).

Man's sin destroyed his relationship with God. Sinful man believes he has no need to depend on Him, and thus feels no obligation to be loyal to Him. Instead of regarding all things as "for God" and "through Him," a person outside of Christ is self-centered. Paul describes this type of person: "For although they knew God, they neither glorified him as God nor gave thanks to him, but their thinking became futile and their foolish hearts were darkened" (Romans 1:21). The Lord Jesus came to bring us back to God. By His death He delivered us from the power of sin, and by His life He showed us how we should live for God and through God.

All for God, all through God. What an impact this attitude will have on your life and mine. Only as we are emptied of self and become wholly dependent on the Lord, will we recognize that all is for God because all is through God. The author and leader of our salvation came to reveal God and His claim upon us. He came to show us that to know Him as Savior and Lord, and to honor Him in our daily walk, is the path to joy. Andrew Murray writes, "Christ came to give us an entirely new conception of what true life is, to show us a new way of thinking and living; to teach us that a heavenly life consists in giving up everything that has the slightest connection with sin for the sake of pleasing the Father perfectly."[1]

Where Am I Going?

"Both the one who makes men holy and those who are made holy are of the same family. So Jesus is not ashamed to call them brothers. He says, 'I will declare your name to my brothers; in the presence of the congregation I will sing your praises.' And again, 'I will put my trust in him.' And again he says, 'Here am I, and the children God has given me'" (Hebrews 2:11-13). Jesus shares with us a descent from Adam. He is qualified to be our Priest and Savior because He shares our nature. This enables Him to call us "brothers."

Usually when we read the word "holy" in the Bible, we think of persons or things separated or consecrated to the Lord. But here in the letter to the Hebrews, the words "those who are made holy" convey another meaning—that of identification with Christ. This oneness of believers in Christ is an amazing truth (see John 17:16,21). The redeemed bear the image and likeness of their Redeemer; holiness marks their oneness. To be holy means to be wholly possessed by God and to walk in fellowship with Him. We are conformed to the image of Christ by accepting His perfect sacrifice for sin, by being filled with the knowledge of His will, and by walking worthy of our Savior through the power of His Spirit within us. So He acknowledges us as one with Himself and calls us His brothers and sisters.

The next verse, "He says, 'I will declare your name to my brothers; in the presence of the congregation I will sing your praises'" (Hebrews 2:12), is quoted from Psalm 22:22. Christ is speaking to the Father and says He will proclaim the Father's name to His brothers. Prior to the resurrection, our Lord never called His followers "brothers;" He called them disciples and friends. But when He was raised, He said to Mary, "Go to my brothers" (John 20:17). He is not ashamed to call us brothers and sisters; may it be our prayer that we never disappoint Him.

Hebrews 2:14-15 continues, "Since the children have flesh and blood, he too shared in their humanity so that by his death he might destroy him who holds the power of death—that is, the devil—and free those who all their lives were held in slavery by their fear of death." One important reason why Christ for a season became lower than angels is that the He had to become flesh and blood in order to become "one" with those He made holy. He had to truly become human.

---

1. Andrew Murray. *The Holiest of All: An Exposition of the Epistle to the Hebrews* (Revell)

The purpose of Jesus Christ's coming and taking on the nature of man was that through death He might destroy Satan, also called the devil, who "holds the power of death." God alone controls life and death, but Satan exercises power within the realm of death, and Christ defeated Satan within that realm. Christ's death on the cross was a stumbling block to many; it looked like a complete defeat. But the Holy Spirit teaches here that in reality Christ's death was a glorious victory. By His death, the Savior overthrew the devil and stripped him of his power of death. When Christ was made sin for us, the power of Satan was destroyed. Sin is paid for by the sacrifice of the Lamb of God; the law has been satisfied (see 2 Corinthians 5:21).

Christ's death gave assurance that believers no longer need fear spiritual death. Many non-Christians will not admit to fear of God's judgment upon sin, usually because they have only a vague idea of who God is. Adam and Eve were afraid and they hid themselves (see Genesis 3:8-10). Felix was frightened as he listened to the truth from the apostle Paul (see Acts 24:25). Christ has delivered us from this bondage. Instead of fear, He is willing to continually fill our hearts with joy and peace. When we stand before God, we will be dressed in Christ's righteousness, "without stain or wrinkle or any other blemish, but holy and blameless" (Ephesians 5:27). Have you personally received Jesus' forgiveness for sin? (See Ephesians 2:8-9.) Then claim the joy and peace that Christ wants to give you daily! Let Him cast out your fear and replace it with His great love and power.

The One Who Rescues Us

"For surely it is not angels he helps, but Abraham's descendants. For this reason he had to be made like his brothers in every way, in order that he might become a merciful and faithful high priest in service to God, and that he might make atonement for the sins of the people" (Hebrews 2:16-17).

The Greek verb here translated "helps" is also rendered "takes on" or "takes hold of." It describes one stretching out his hand and rescuing another. One of the mysteries is why fallen angels were not given "help" (see Matthew 25:41). This we must leave with God who does all things well and according to His sovereign will. The author of Hebrews again speaks of Christ taking on the nature of man, so that He could redeem man. He reemphasizes that the Lord Jesus must so unite Himself with those He would ransom that their sins would become His sins. He not only took our place on the cross; He became one with us.

The Lord Jesus now is a "merciful and faithful high priest," merciful toward man and faithful to God. He is tender, loving, compassionate, and sympathetic. But all His dealings with us meet the requirements of God's holiness. The sacrificial work of the Savior on the cross perfectly satisfied the holiness and justice of God. If you know Christ as your Savior, your sins are blotted out forever (see Acts 3:19; Psalm 51:7-10). We will have opportunity later for detailed study of Christ's sacrificial death and His high priestly office.

This chapter ends on a note that is a source of encouragement and comfort to believers. Because Christ "Himself was tempted in that which He has suffered, He is able to come to the aid of those who are tempted" (Hebrews 2:18). He suffered when tempted; He never yielded. It is when we resist Satan's attacks that we suffer. But Jesus Christ is able and will help us. Nothing you will experience is unknown to Him. His temptations weren't confined to the one time we read about in Scripture (see Matthew 4:1-11). He met other temptations throughout His earthly life. He knows how to rescue the godly from temptation (see 2 Peter 2:9). He is the Victor, and if you and He are one, you too are victorious! (See 1 John 5:4-5.) Thanks be to God!

Study Questions

Before you begin your study this week:
- Pray and ask God to speak to you through His Holy Spirit.
- Use only the Bible for your answers.
- Write down your answers and the verses you used.
- Answer the "Challenge" questions if you have the time and want to do them.
- Share your answers to the "Personal" questions with the class only if you want to share them.

First Day: Read the Commentary on Hebrews 2:5-18.

1. What meaningful or new thought did you find in the commentary on Hebrews 2:5-18 or from your teacher's lecture? What personal application did you choose to apply to your life?

2. Look for a verse in the lesson to memorize this week. Write it down, carry it with you, or post it in a prominent place. Make a real effort to learn the verse and its "address" (reference of where it is found in the Bible).

Second Day: Read Hebrews 3, concentrating on verse 1.

1. What does the author call his readers in Hebrews 3:1?   *Brother or Sister ...*

2. a. The word "holy" means that Christians are set apart for the service of God. Who initiates this service according to Hebrews 3:1?

   b. What do you learn about this in the following Scriptures?

      2 Timothy 1:9

      1 Peter 2:9

3. On whom does the author of Hebrews say believers should focus? (Hebrews 3:1b)

4. a. Challenge: This is the only place in the New Testament that calls Jesus an "apostle." Look up this word in a dictionary or Bible dictionary. How does it appropriately describe Jesus and His ministry?

b. Challenge: What else does Hebrews 3:1 call Jesus, in addition to "apostle"? What aspect of His work does this description bring to mind?

High Priest did but nat @nought what Jesus want.

5. Hebrews 3:1 says that, as believers, we "confess" Jesus. What does this mean, according to Romans 10:9-10?

6. Personal: Have you confessed Jesus as your Lord? If so, are you fixing your thoughts on Him? What would be different in your life if you were able to do this consistently?

Third Day: Review Hebrews 3, concentrating on verses 2-6.

1. To whom does the author of Hebrews now compare Jesus?

2. Moses was regarded by the Jews as the greatest of men. But the author of Hebrews is not merely citing human opinion. Read Numbers 12:5-8. Who declared this fact about Moses?

 *God himself*

3. a. What analogy does the writer give to show why Jesus is worthy of greater honor than Moses? (Hebrews 3:3)

b. The author interrupts his argument here to make a point that he does not want us to lose sight of. Who made everything and therefore is over all? (Hebrews 3:4)

God.

4. How does Hebrews 3:5-6a compare Moses and Christ in another way?

Trust

5. a. Who makes up God's house? (Hebrews 3:6b)

b. What demonstrates that we are truly part of God's house? (Hebrews 3:6c)

Being part of God's house.

6. Personal: Do you sometimes feel that your courage to follow Jesus is failing? Read 1 Peter 1:3-5. What does verse 5 say is the source of your ability to hold on to your courage? When you feel weak, remember whose power is upholding you.

God give rest prest, heaven rest. our rest is eternal rest.

Fourth Day: Review Hebrews 3, concentrating on verses 7-11.

1. After comparing Jesus with Moses, the author of Hebrews now compares their followers, quoting from Psalm 95:7-11. What did the people of Israel do that followers of Christ should not repeat? (Hebrews 3:7-11)

2. Challenge: To "harden" the heart is to disobey the voice of God and act in accordance with one's own desires.[1] Read Exodus 17:1-7, which describes the incident to which the psalmist refers in Psalm 95:8 (Hebrews 3:8). How did Israel rebel and test the Lord?

Moshe wear the lord and they complain: no water. God said hit stone by stick. They didn't sees @ spritu eyes.

3. Israel's faithlessness was not just demonstrated during this one incident. How long did their faithlessness last? (Hebrews 3:9; Psalm 95:9-10a)

4. a. How will God always react to sin? (Hebrews 3:10a)

    b. What two things characterized Israel's sin? (Hebrews 3:10b)

1. *The Expositor's Bible Commentary*

5. a. What is the result when a person refuses to take the trouble to learn about God and to act in obedience upon what they learn? (Hebrews 3:11)

never enter with rest. Unity with God never.

b. Challenge: In this passage the psalmist refers to an incident near the end of Israel's 40-year wilderness period. Read Numbers 13:1-2, 25-33; 14:1-11, 20-24, and summarize this incident.

6. Personal: Hebrews 3:7 began its warning with, "*Today*, if you hear his voice..." (italics added). Is God trying to get your attention today? Have you been putting off dealing with some issue, or taking some action to which He is calling you? What is your attitude toward the things He is telling you?

Pray.

Fifth Day: Review Hebrews 3, concentrating on verses 12-14.

1. What is the inevitable action of a sinful, unbelieving heart? (Hebrew 3:12)

2. a. What are we to do for one another? (Hebrews 3:13)

b. Read Ephesians 4:22-24. Where do sin's deceitful desires stem from in our lives? How can we avoid being hardened by sin's deceitfulness?

3. What does the author assert in Hebrews 3:14?

4. Read John 10:27-29. Who enables us to "hold firmly till the end the confidence we had at first"?

5. Personal: Do you realize how important your encouragement is for other believers, and how much you need to receive it from them? Whom do you need to encourage today? Who has been encouraging you?

Sixth Day: Review Hebrews 3, concentrating on verses 15-19.

1. The writer now goes back and summarizes his point. What characterized the people that Moses led out of Egypt? (Hebrews 3:16)

2. What happened to those who aroused God's anger through continued rebellion? (Hebrews 3:17)

3. To whom did God swear that they would never enter His rest? (Hebrews 3:18)

4. What prevented them from entering His rest? (Hebrews 3:19)

5. The people of Israel had every reason to expect that they would enter God's rest in the promised land after He led them out of Egypt. Yet they "were *not able* to enter." This was not God's arbitrary punishment, but rather the inevitable outcome of their unbelief and disobedience. Read John 14:15 and Matthew 11:28-29. What does Jesus say we must do in order to find rest?

6. Personal: Just as He did for Israel, God has done so much for you. Are you willing to submit your will to His so that you may enter His rest?

Hebrews
Lesson 6

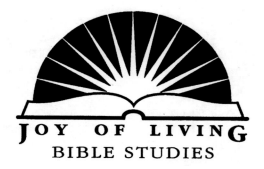

JOY OF LIVING
BIBLE STUDIES

Hebrews 3

Can you imagine yourself as a Hebrew Christian receiving this letter? You've just read that Christ is a merciful and faithful high priest. Your background has given you a high regard for the Levitical priesthood.[1] You know that the high priest represented Israel when he went into the Most Holy Place, the place of God's presence (see Exodus 26:33-34; 28:29-30). Now Christ is your access to God. You are reminded that Christ became man and is the perfect sacrifice for sin, dying in your place. Ever since you received this letter you've been rehearsing in your mind what you read about Christ being better than the prophets, and even superior to angels. You rejoice in the redemption that is yours in the Lord Jesus. Beyond that is His sympathy and identification with you in all your trials and temptations.

You read on. "Therefore...fix your thoughts on Jesus" (Hebrews 3:1). What does this mean? Didn't you give some thought to Him when you heard of His miraculous birth, His ministry, His death and resurrection, and then the wonder of His ascension? What more is there? Let's discover what the Holy Spirit says in Hebrews 3 to you and to all believers.

Christ Greater Than Moses

We read, "Therefore, holy brothers, who share in the heavenly calling, fix your thoughts on Jesus, the apostle and high priest whom we confess" (Hebrews 3:1). The Hebrew Christians are greeted as brothers because they belong to the family of God. "Holy brothers" distinguishes them from unbelieving Jews. The term applies to all who receive Christ by faith and call God their Father, to those who "share in the heavenly calling." The Christian's calling originates in heaven—it is God who has called us to be His own.

To fix our thoughts on Jesus means to thoroughly ponder who and what He is, to think about His authority, His glory, His excellence. Our hearts should be constantly rejoicing in Him. There are so many demands on our time that some who profess Jesus' name give Him only an occasional thought. Many fail to come to a fuller knowledge of the Lord by fixing their thoughts on Him. This explains why so many

Christians have only a vague sense of who He is and so never claim all that they possess as children of the Heavenly King. Psalm 37:4 says, "Delight yourself in the LORD and he will give you the desires of your heart."

Hebrews 3:1 calls Jesus "the apostle," the only time this term is used for Jesus in the Bible. Apostle means, "a person sent by another; a messenger; envoy"[2] or "one sent on a mission."[3] Many years ago the king of Syria, Antiochus Epiphanes, invaded Egypt. Rome sent an envoy named Popillius to stop him. When Popillius caught up with Antiochus Epiphanes they spoke with each other for a time, for they were friends. Finally Antiochus asked Popillius why he had come. The envoy answered that he had come with a message from Rome to abandon the invasion and go home. "I will consider it," said Antiochus. Popillius drew a circle in the sand around the Syrian king. "Consider it," he said, "and come to your decision before you leave that circle." Antiochus thought a minute, then said, "Very well, I will go home." Popillius had no army and he used no force. But behind him was the power and authority of the Roman empire. The Lord Jesus came from God and with God's authority. In Him God speaks. All God's grace and love and power are in Christ, your apostle (see John 17:2-3).

Jesus is also called the "high priest whom we confess" (Hebrews 3:1). The word *priest* comes from the Latin "pontiff," meaning bridge builder. The Lord Jesus Christ bridges the gap between man and God. He speaks to God for man and to man for God. Jesus is the perfect high priest. He is the only one through whom man can come to God (see 1 Timothy 2:5).

Jesus "was faithful to the one who appointed him, just as Moses was faithful in all God's house" (Hebrews 3:2). Moses was loved and respected by the Jewish people. His was a unique place in the history of Israel. God's hand was upon him throughout his life. Rescued by the king's daughter from Pharaoh's plot to kill every son born to the Hebrews, he was trained in the king's house. Thus God prepared him for the great work He had for him. Moses was a faithful servant of God as he led the Israelites from Egyptian bondage to the land of promise. He was God's mouthpiece; he was Israel's representative. The Jews knew that their Scriptures said that God spoke in visions to the prophets but that to Moses He spoke face to face (see Numbers 12:5-8). It was incredible to think that anyone ever was closer to God than Moses. Hebrews 3:2 speaks of the similarity of Christ and Moses as

---

1. The term "Levitical priesthood" refers to the system for service in the Tabernacle that God set up in the time of Moses. Aaron, the high priest, was a member of the tribe of Levi. The "priests" were those Levites who were the descendants of Aaron, and the "Levites" included all those who belonged to the tribe of Levi, whether or not they were descendants of Aaron.

2. M.G. Easton M.A., D.D., *Illustrated Bible Dictionary*, Third Edition, published by Thomas Nelson, 1897. Public Domain.
3. *Merriam-Webster Online Dictionary*, 2009.

to their faithfulness, before it shows how Christ is superior to Israel's great leader and deliverer. Moses was a great man of God—but he was still only human. Jesus is God, and He never fails in His care for the family of God (see 2 Thessalonians 3:3; Hebrews 10:23).

Next we read, "Jesus has been found worthy of greater honor than Moses, just as the builder of a house has greater honor than the house itself" (Hebrews 3:3). The first evidence presented is that Christ is the builder of God's house, meaning He is the founder of God's family and is at the head of God's family. Moses could not claim this distinction. He did not originate the house of Israel; he was simply a member. He could not make people children of God as Christ did. Israel as a nation already belonged to God by covenant relationship. Christ came to people dead in sin, separated from God, and made them new creatures (see 2 Corinthians 5:17; Ephesians 2:10). Moses was a great man, a man of God, a notable leader, commended by the Lord as faithful. He had more than a casual knowledge of God. But Jesus *is* God (see John 1:1-18). Upon this truth is established the superiority of the Lord Jesus.

The letter comes to the crucial point: "Moses was faithful as a *servant* in all God's house, testifying to what would be said in the future. But Christ is faithful as a *son* over God's house" (Hebrews 3:5-6a, italics added). These verses tell us at least two things that confirm Christ's higher position. While Moses was a servant in God's family, Christ is the Son who is head over the family. True, Moses was honored in that he was entrusted with the care of the whole house of Israel. But the family of the faithful Son includes Jews and Gentiles alike who have trusted Him as Savior. As Christ was a faithful Son, so He calls all Christians to faithfulness in their commitment to the Lord. Faithfulness should characterize our daily lives (see 2 Timothy 2:1-15).

Hebrews 3:6 finishes, "And we are his house, if we hold on to our courage and the hope of which we boast." We will suffer trial and temptation. Satan delights in testing God's children (see 1 Peter 5:8-9). We must hold on to our courage and hope, yet our security is not based upon the strength of our faith. Peter wrote, "Through faith [we] are shielded *by God's power* until the coming of the salvation that is ready to be revealed in the last time" (1 Peter 1:5, italics added).

The writer of Hebrews wanted to be sure that the Hebrew believers were firmly established in the faith and that they would continue to grow in grace and in the knowledge of the Savior. If they were drifting away and neglecting spiritual things, it wasn't too late for them to fix their thoughts on Jesus and recommit their lives to Him.

There May Be No Tomorrow

The writer of Hebrews quotes from Psalm 95, continuing the backward look: "So, as the Holy Spirit says: 'Today, if you hear his voice, do not harden your hearts as you did in the rebellion, during the time of testing in the desert, where your fathers tested and tried me and for forty years saw what I did. That is why I was angry with that generation, and I said, "Their hearts are always going astray, and they have not known my ways." So I declared on oath in my anger, "They shall never enter my rest"'" (Hebrews 3:7-11).

Israel tested and tried God for forty years in the desert. When Moses recounted their experiences he declared, "You have been rebellious against the LORD ever since I have known you." (Deuteronomy 9:24). Because that generation of Israel willfully refused to walk in obedience to the Lord, they never learned His ways.

The repetition of the words of Psalm 95 in this letter to believers serves as a severe warning. As far as that generation of Israel was concerned, God's patience was exhausted. The sentence He pronounced was final: They were denied entrance into the promised land. Think of the high hopes of those who came out of Egypt's bondage, now never to be realized. Think of the wasted years! Every day in the wilderness was a gift from their heavenly Father, who invited them over and over again to obey Him and receive His blessing. What joy would have been theirs to live in their own land, to come at last to a place of rest—God's rest. No more weary hours of pitching tents, gathering manna, packing up to move on and trudging through the endless, dusty, rocky wastes to another campsite. But they never made it.

Theirs was an awesome penalty. But God does not wink at sin. Many people seem to think that while God's promises are unfailing, His judgment can be evaded. John the Baptist testified, "Whoever believes in the Son has eternal life, but whoever rejects the Son will not see life, for God's wrath remains on him" (John 3:36).

The readers of this letter knew of the unbelief and disobedience of their ancestors. The ancient Hebrews' hearts had become calloused. Instead of praising God for their deliverance from Egyptian bondage, they were grumbling and complaining. God had been gracious to them, had supplied their needs, had protected them and had led them forth by the right way. Yet, when He brought them to the borders of the promised land, they refused to go in. Their fear of the dangers in the land overwhelmed what faith they had in God (see Numbers 13:25—14:10). And so He decreed they should not enter into His rest. They never made it into Canaan, but died in the desert, leaving the task of occupying the land to their children who had been under the age of accountability when the people stopped at the border (see Numbers 14:22-38).

God offered the Hebrews the promised land. He offers us a life of blessing far beyond what the Israelites could experience. But He asks that we put our trust in Him and believe His promises. Obedience is necessary. God's blessings come to those who believe His word and obey His instructions. This is the day to trust Him for salvation (see John 5:24). *Now* is the time to choose to do what you know the Lord is asking of you. Remember, there may be no tomorrow.

Me, a Pseudo-Christian?

The letter to the Hebrews has nearly exhausted expressions of warning. Readers are advised to pay attention and not to slip away from the truth or neglect the means of grace God has given. The author points out the spiritual gain in thinking about the Lord and considering His mercies daily. We are assured that our confidence and our hope will be unshaken because our hope is in Christ.

Those who call themselves Christians, but whose profession is not genuine, are addressed next: "See to it, brothers, that none of you has a sinful, unbelieving heart that turns away from the living God" (Hebrews 3:12). An evil, unbelieving heart is one occupied with self. It is taken up with worldliness and has put out of mind any thought of the Lord or His Word. The person whose heart is described thus has turned away from God. Outwardly he or she may still profess a belief and attend a church. But unbelief marks the evil heart; and unbelief renders a man or woman incapable of fellowship with the living God. In the Old Testament when God was spoken of as the living God, it was in contrast to idols that could neither speak nor hear. There are professing Christians who do not bow before images of wood or stone, but they worship idols they have chosen that take the place of the living God. They have turned a deaf ear to God who has spoken in His Son.

Keep in mind that unbelieving Jews were urging the Hebrew Christians to renounce Christ and return to Judaism and the one true God. But the writer of Hebrews has established that Christ *is* God. Now he warns that abandoning faith in Christ and returning to Judaism would not be going back to the one true God, but rather departing from Him. Christ is the true and living God, as confirmed in Hebrews 1 and 2. The one thing we need to have in order to receive the blessing and fullness of God is a heart of faith (see Ephesians 3:17-19). Paul wrote, "For it is with your heart that you believe and are justified, and it is with your mouth that you confess and are saved" (Romans 10:10).

The letter continues, "But encourage one another daily, as long as it is called Today, so that none of you may be hardened by sin's deceitfulness" (Hebrews 3:13). The word "encourage" may also be translated "warn," meaning to call attention to. Christians are called to be concerned for each other (see 1 Corinthians 12:25), to love one another (see John 13:34), to pray for each other (see James 5:16), to instruct one another (see Romans 15:14) and to build each other up (see 1 Thessalonians 5:11). When we love, care and pray for fellow believers we are in a position to instruct or warn them. Others need your expressions of love and concern. Many are hurting, lonely, frustrated. Too often we criticize a Christian's failures, discussing his or her problems with others, rather than speaking directly to the person and offering to help. Your encouragement may be the turning point in another's life.

Hebrews 3:13 says that sin is deceitful. Some sin may seem insignificant. Habit or custom makes some sin seem legitimate. Believers can be caught up in the deceitfulness of sin. It can be seen in an unloving spirit, backbiting, pride, or "little" lies. Many people think of sin as some heinous crime, such as murder. Scripture tells us that there are sins of omission (see James 4:17) and even sins of ignorance (see Leviticus 5:17). Sin is disobedience to what God has told us in His Word; it is anything we allow to come between us and the Savior.

The apostle John revealed the remedy for sin: "If we confess our sins, he is faithful and just and will forgive us our sins and purify us from all unrighteousness" (1 John 1:9). Recognize these "little" sins that mar your fellowship with God, that keep you from spending time in prayer and in the Word. Confess them and put them out of your life so you do not become so accustomed to them that you are calloused and unwilling to forsake them. Even things that in themselves are good may be crowding out what the Lord has for you to do. Ask the Lord to help you arrange your priorities according to His will.

"We have come to share in Christ" (Hebrews 3:14). This is a treasure conferred upon believers when they receive Him as Savior. We are inclined to think of ourselves, if we are believers, as saved by His precious blood, made heirs with Christ, but somehow detached from Him. We know that the Lord Jesus represents us before His Father in heaven. He is both our intercessor and our high priest. The glorious truth is that we are so joined to the Lord as to be one with Him, truly a mystery of God's grace. Our oneness with Him enables us to live a life worthy of our high calling in Christ Jesus. He will have first place in our lives; our thoughts and actions will conform to His will. A life so lived gives evidence of the genuineness of our profession of faith; this is what it means to "hold firmly till the end the confidence we had at first" (Hebrews 3:14).

Again the writer of Hebrews repeats his plea to "do not harden your hearts," to "hear His voice" (Hebrews 3:15). The Lord speaks tenderly to you. He speaks in the Son who died that you might have eternal life. Will you receive Him as your Savior and Lord today? (See John 3:16.) He speaks in love to you who have drifted dangerously close to disaster. His invitation is to come to the throne of grace to obtain help and mercy (see Hebrews 4:16; 1 John 1:8-9). Come back to Him and be filled and renewed. Hear Him who knows the secrets of your heart, who says, "Come to me" (Matthew 11:28). He will give you peace and joy, and rest. Do it today. Tomorrow may never dawn.

Study Questions

Before you begin your study this week:
- ❧ Pray and ask God to speak to you through His Holy Spirit.
- ❧ Use only the Bible for your answers.
- ❧ Write down your answers and the verses you used.
- ❧ Answer the "Challenge" questions if you have the time and want to do them.
- ❧ Share your answers to the "Personal" questions with the class only if you want to share them.

First Day: Read the Commentary on Hebrews 3.

1. What meaningful or new thought did you find in the commentary on Hebrews 3 or from your teacher's lecture? What personal application did you choose to apply to your life?

2. Look for a verse in the lesson to memorize this week. Write it down, carry it with you, or post it in a prominent place. Make a real effort to learn the verse and its "address" (reference of where it is found in the Bible).

Second Day: Read Hebrews 4, concentrating on verses 1-4.

1. a. Although the generation of Israel that left Egypt disobeyed God and failed to enter the land of promise, what promise of God still stands? (Hebrews 4:1a)

   b. What warning is given to us? (Hebrews 4:1b)

2. How must we act upon the message we have heard—the gospel—so that we are not "found to have fallen short of it"? (Hebrews 4:2)

3. When did God's rest begin? (Hebrews 4:3)

4. The writer of Hebrews goes on to quote from Genesis 2:2 to support his point. Compare this passage with Hebrews 4:4.

5. Challenge: God's rest began when He completed creation, and the man and woman He created enjoyed that state of rest in the Garden of Eden. What happened that removed Adam and his descendants from this state of rest? Read Genesis 3:17-19.

6. Personal: Sinful humanity's condition is the opposite of rest: Life is hard. Many religions teach that in order to reach a condition of rest, a person must do good works; in fact, that's what many people think that Christianity teaches. But that couldn't be farther from the truth. As Hebrews 4:2 tells us, all we need to do to receive God's rest is to have faith in the message He has sent us through Jesus Christ. Have you stopped trying by your own good works to reach God's rest?

Third Day: Review Hebrews 4, concentrating on verses 5-7.

1. What very important points does the author of Hebrews again repeat in Hebrews 4:5-6?

2. God prepared a rest for humanity to enter into, but those originally invited did not enter in. Yet, He says, some will enter that rest. Read Matthew 22:1-10. How does Jesus' parable express this same theme?

3. Challenge: The writer of Hebrews concentrated on two generations only—the wilderness generation and his contemporaries. He was not arguing that no Israelite ever entered God's rest, only that the wilderness generation was denied entry because of its disobedience. Many Israelites before and after the time of Christ did choose to believe God's promises and enter His rest. Read Ephesians 2:11-16. How does Paul say that God extended His invitation beyond Israel?

4. Given the facts as the writer of Hebrews has set them out in Hebrews 4:5-6, what opportunity and decision does every person in every generation face? (Hebrews 4:7)

5. Personal: Who do you know that is "without hope and without God in the world" (Ephesians 2:12)? You may be the way God chooses to speak to that person, to offer them hope in Him. Write down here what you want to say to that person. If you are afraid, or do not know what to say, ask God to give you the words—He will do it!

Fourth Day: Review Hebrews 4, concentrating on verses 8-10.

1. What does the writer of Hebrews observe about Joshua in Hebrews 4:8?

2. Challenge: Read Joshua 1:1-6 and 23:1-3. Did Joshua lead Israel into the promised land?

3. Israel's entry into Canaan under Joshua was a partial and temporary entering of God's rest.[1] But this was not the kind of rest that David had in mind in Psalm 95, nor the kind the writer of Hebrews had in this chapter. What kind of rest remains to be entered by God's people? (Hebrews 4:9)

4. How is this rest described in Hebrews 4:10?

5. a. When a person enters God's rest, he or she stops trying to earn God's favor by doing good works, and instead rests securely in what Christ has done. How does Ephesians 2:8-9 express this?

   b. Once we have entered God's rest, what does Ephesians 2:10 say we are created and enabled to do?

6. Personal: Have you learned to rest in Christ's work, and stop striving to earn God's favor by your own works? How has that changed your attitude towards doing good works?

---

1. *The NIV Study Bible.*

Fifth Day: Review Hebrews 4, concentrating on verses 11-13.

1. What does the writer urge his readers in Hebrews 4:11?

2. Challenge: Read 1 Corinthians 10:1-12. How did Paul refer to Israel's wilderness generation to make a similar point?

3. How does Hebrews 4:12 describe the word of God—the revelation of God?

4. Is there anything in our being that we can hide from God? (Hebrews 4:13)

5. What do you learn about this from the following verses?

   Jeremiah 17:10

   John 5:28-29

   1 Corinthians 4:5

6. Personal: Are there thoughts or actions in your life that you wish to hide from other people? Do you sometimes feel that you are also hiding them from God? How do you feel when you realize He sees it all? How does 1 John 1:9-10 help you deal with these hidden things in your life?

Sixth Day: Review Hebrews 4, concentrating on verses 14-16.

1. How is Jesus described in Hebrews 4:14?

2. Why is Jesus able to sympathize with us? (Hebrews 4:15)

3. You may think that Jesus, being sinless, didn't really have to battle temptation very hard. But the fact is that in every way that He was tempted, He would not yield—He fought the full force of each temptation and won the victory over it. We, who are sinners, often give in before the full force of the temptation has washed over us. Read Luke 4:1-13. This was certainly not the only time or the last time Jesus would be tempted. How does verse 13 show this?

4. Because of Jesus' power as a great high priest and His sympathy for us as a man, what are believers able to do? (Hebrews 4:16)

5. Personal: How does it make you feel to know that Jesus fought successfully through every kind of temptation that you will ever encounter? What temptation do you face right now? He has been there and won the victory. Now He offers you mercy and grace to help you as you face this situation. If you would like to, write a prayer here about your problem, asking for His help.

Hebrews
Lesson 7

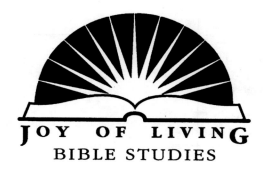

JOY OF LIVING
BIBLE STUDIES

Hebrews 4

Every Hebrew knew the history of Israel's deliverance from Egypt and the subsequent forty-year wilderness journey. Their rejection of the spies' report at Kadesh Barnea had sealed their doom (see Deuteronomy 1). "Who made God angry?" "Why couldn't they go into the promised land?" Questions such as these at the close of chapter 3 were intended to stir up the conscience of the reader. They served to remind Hebrew believers of the unbelief and rebellion of their ancestors, notwithstanding God's provision, protection and providential care.

God's judgment was severe. With the exception of Caleb and Joshua, who believed God and urged that the people enter the land without fear of the Canaanites, God decreed that all the adults who came out of Egypt should die in the desert. God's promises had not failed, but because that generation didn't trust Him, they never entered into His promised rest.

Don't Miss God's Rest!

God's "rest" is mentioned many times in this passage. In Hebrews 4:1 we see that "the promise of entering his rest still stands," and we do not want to "be found to have fallen short of it." Then in Hebrews 4:3 we read, "We who have believed enter that rest," yet God said of the unbelieving generation of Israel, "They shall never enter my rest." Next in verse 4 the writer mentions the rest of God following the six days of creation: His work was finished, and "on the seventh day God rested from all his work." This "rest" was in recognition of His complete and perfect work.

At the time the letter to the Hebrews was written, Israel had long since occupied the Land, and they had been observing the Sabbaths for generations. Why, then, is the writer pressing this matter of entering God's rest? Neither the occupation of the land nor the observance of the Sabbath is what David meant in Psalm 95 nor what the author of Hebrews means.

Obviously, the promise of this rest was not yet fulfilled. Four hundred years after Israel entered Canaan, David was still speaking of that rest to people living there. Simply living in Canaan didn't bring them into God's rest. God's rest is spiritual rather than physical. After He had finished six days of creation, on the seventh day He began a rest that hasn't ended. This doesn't mean that God is not occupied with the affairs of the universe, that He is not mindful of you and me and the smallest detail of our lives. He rests from His creative acts, but He never rests from governing His universe. His watchful care of His own continues day and night (see John 5:17).

If Israel under Joshua's leadership had known and experienced all that the word *rest* implies, then God would not have spoken of another day, "Today" (Hebrews 4:7). Israel's rest in the Promised Land was an earthly inheritance. Far different is the believer's promised rest in Christ: "Come to me, all you who are weary and burdened, and I will give you rest. Take my yoke upon you and learn from me, for I am gentle and humble in heart, and you will find rest for your souls" (Matthew 11:28-29). Christ's rest exceeds that into which Joshua led Israel. Hebrew believers could see that Christ is indeed superior to Joshua.

The believer's rest begins when he or she stops trusting in his or her own work and rests instead in the finished work of Christ. "However, to the man who does not work but trusts God who justifies the wicked, his faith is credited as righteousness" (Romans 4:5).

God tells us the promise of His rest still stands. Note that this rest is not something God *gives*; it is His own rest into which we may *enter* (see Hebrews 4:1). And how do we enter? Hebrews 4:2 says, "For we also have had the gospel preached to us, just as they did; but the message they heard was of no value to them, because *those who heard did not combine it with faith*" (italics added). Knowing, and even believing, the truths of God is not enough. Our knowledge and belief must be combined with faith, which puts our knowledge and belief into action. Ray Stedman explains it this way,

> We share in Christ if that faith which began continues to produce in us that which faith alone can produce, the fruit of the Spirit. This is the second warning of this book [Hebrews]. The first one was against drifting—the danger of paying no attention, of sitting in a meeting and letting the words flow by while our minds are occupied elsewhere; the peril of letting these magnificent truths, which alone have power to set men free, to drift by, unheeded, unheard.

> But this second warning is against the danger of hardening—of hearing the words and believing them, understanding what they mean, but of taking no action upon them. The peril of holding truth in the head, but never letting it get into the heart. But truth known never does anything; it is truth done which sets us free.

Truth known simply puffs us up in pride of knowledge. We can quote the Scriptures by the yard, can memorize it, can know the message of every book and know the whole book from cover to cover, but truth known will never do anything for us. It is truth done, truth acted upon, that moves and delivers and changes.

The terrible danger, which the writer is pointing out, is that truth that is known but not acted on has an awful effect of hardening the heart so that it is no longer able to act—and we lose the ability to believe.[1]

"Therefore," says the writer of Hebrews, "God again set a certain day, calling it Today, when a long time later he spoke through David, as was said before: 'Today, if you hear his voice, do not harden your hearts'" (Hebrews 4:7). Don't let your heart become hardened by ignoring the truth you are learning. Let God lead you into His rest by willingly making Him your Lord, allowing Him to make you more and more like Christ each day, through the work of His Holy Spirit within you.

It's Alive and It Speaks

The writer of Hebrews repeats his warning, including himself with his readers, "Let us, therefore, make every effort to enter that rest, so that no one will fall by following their example of disobedience" (Hebrews 4:11). Then he goes on to tell us what guide we should follow as we make every effort to enter God's rest: "For the word of God is living and active. Sharper than any double-edged sword, it penetrates even to dividing soul and spirit, joints and marrow; it judges the thoughts and attitudes of the heart" (Hebrews 4:12).

The Word is sharp, alive, and active. It is living and vital. It is for all people and for all time. Every person must either accept or reject its commands and its offer of eternal life. The Word of God, when applied by the Holy Spirit to the Christian, is like the surgeon's knife that wounds in order to heal.

The Word of God exposes our innermost secrets. It is able to judge the thoughts and attitudes of the heart. Unbelievers recognize their awful sinfulness and wretchedness only when these are revealed to them by the Word of God and the Holy Spirit. The Word searches the heart of the believer and reveals his need of daily cleansing and a closer walk with the Lord. As we continue in fellowship with Him, His Word comes to us not only as a sword, but also as a lamp that lights our path and guides us in God's ways (see Psalm 119:105).

In summary, the writer says, "Nothing in all creation is hidden from God's sight. Everything is uncovered and laid bare before the eyes of him to whom we must give account" (Hebrews 4:13). None of our trappings and disguises, none of our pretenses will benefit us when we stand in God's presence. Even as He speaks to us now, He knows our response, for He looks on our hearts and sees the motive that prompts our conduct (see 1 Samuel 16:7).

---

1. Ray C. Stedman. "Living out of Rest." http://www.raystedman.org/hebrews1/0086.html.

Our Great High Priest

The closing words of Hebrews 4 tell of the provisions of God's grace while we are in places of trial: "Therefore, since we have a great high priest who has gone through the heavens, Jesus the Son of God, let us hold firmly to the faith we profess. For we do not have a high priest who is unable to sympathize with our weaknesses, but we have one who has been tempted in every way, just as we are—yet was without sin. Let us then approach the throne of grace with confidence, so that we may receive mercy and find grace to help us in our time of need" (Hebrews 4:14-16). These verses give us assurance and encouragement as we "press on towards the goal" (Philippians 3:14), being certain by faith that we have entered God's rest.

In earthly things all of us enjoy the pleasure of possession. We have a father or mother. We may have children. We have a home, a car, or other material possessions. Christians also have a "great high priest,…Jesus." He is ours; we are His. All He is and has is at our disposal. Each of us needs to trust the Lord Jesus for everything, to experience His greatness and sufficiency. Because he has proved Himself faithful and true, because He lives in heaven for you and me, let us live wholly for Him.

The Lord Jesus Christ is worthy of our total commitment to Him, and we need to thank Him for His constant presence and power in our lives as believers. We need to be sensitive to the Holy Spirit's leading, and willing to give our gentle and joyous witness of God's faithfulness, love, and power whenever we are given an opportunity. Jesus is the Son of God, our great high priest, our risen Lord and Savior.

In Old Testament times, God gave instructions for the building of a tabernacle and later a temple where He was to be worshiped. Aaron and his sons were appointed priests. Daily sacrifices were made and God's order carried out in the feasts and offerings. These animal sacrifices could not atone for man's sin, because "it is impossible for the blood of bulls and goats to take away sins" (Hebrews 10:4). But the temple sacrifices pointed to a future sacrifice that would atone for sin once and for all who would receive it—Christ's own sacrificial death for sin.

After Jesus died on the cross and was buried, He rose again from death into life to sit at God's right hand, there to represent us as our great high priest. No longer was there any need for further sacrifice by mere human priests in a temple. Our high priest, Jesus Christ, was the final and complete Sacrifice, which was offered up once and for all time. All people can share in this sacrifice for sin by coming in simple faith to Christ (see John 3:16-17). Now, as believers, we are brought near to God through the blood of Christ (see Ephesians 2:13).

The glorious truth that our great high priest may be approached by even the weakest believer rests in the fact that He experienced all our weaknesses. Though we are unworthy and sinful, undeserving of the mediation of such a great high priest, the Son of God, we are assured of His sympathetic understanding and His compassion. Nothing can touch the child of God that has not first been felt by our Lord, who lived as a man and suffered every temptation, yet fought the full force of each temptation and won the victory over it. What a comfort to those who suffer affliction, temptation, trials, and pain. Jesus understands every heart's longing. He never wearies of our tears. He reaches out to strengthen, to uphold. He gives "a crown of beauty instead of ashes, the oil of gladness instead of mourning, and a garment of praise instead of a spirit of despair" (Isaiah 61:3).

Our great high priest, God's perfect, holy Son, did not sin. His very nature is holiness. God's Son perfectly obeyed His Father, so that temptation did not result in sin. Temptation is a trial, which may have a good or bad ending. Satan is ever on the trail of the believer to lure us away from the path God has planned for us. He wins a victory when a Christian turns from fellowship with the Lord to a careless, prayerless life. When temptations come, and they do every day, flee to your refuge—to the throne of grace. This is the place where no charges are made against sinners, for you are in Christ, reconciled to God, complete in Him. Come in confidence, with freedom and fearlessness, and Jesus will provide you the strength to resist any temptation (see 1 Corinthians 10:13; 2 Peter 2:9).

In God's presence we "receive mercy and find grace to help us in our time of need" (Hebrews 4:16). We always need mercy to bring us back into close fellowship with the Lord, to cleanse us from sin, to restore to us the joy of our salvation. Mercy is *not* receiving what we deserve. Grace is receiving what we *don't* deserve.

Whatever your need is, God's all-sufficient grace is available. Grace is God's Riches At Christ's Expense. Jesus died so that grace could be available to anyone who would come in faith to Him. Have you come in simple faith to Christ yet? If you have, are you asking Him to show you opportunities to share this "Good News" with those who have not yet heard it explained in a loving, clear way?

When we experience spiritual failure, chances are we have not been spending time with the Lord in prayer, approaching with confidence the throne of grace. Hebrews offers a rich, sustaining relationship with the Lord. It speaks of entering into His very presence in worship and adoration. This joy is yours, this peace of quiet rest, near to the heart of God. Are you experiencing the richness of such a relationship with Christ? Choose to approach Him through prayer and reading His Word daily. Let Him speak to you. Enjoy His fellowship as you enter into His presence!

It is the glow of Jesus Christ within the believer that creates our inward and outward beauty. Christians are like stained glass windows: they sparkle like crystal when yielded to the light of God's Son. When dark times and difficulties come, believers continue to shine only as they are yielded to and dependent on the power and light within them: the Lord Jesus Christ. Is the light of Christ shining through you?

Study Questions

Before you begin your study this week:

- ❧ Pray and ask God to speak to you through His Holy Spirit.
- ❧ Use only the Bible for your answers.
- ❧ Write down your answers and the verses you used.
- ❧ Answer the "Challenge" questions if you have the time and want to do them.
- ❧ Share your answers to the "Personal" questions with the class only if you want to share them.

First Day: Read the Commentary on Hebrews 4.

1. What meaningful or new thought did you find in the commentary on Hebrews 4 or from your teacher's lecture? What personal application did you choose to apply to your life?

2. Look for a verse in the lesson to memorize this week. Write it down, carry it with you, or post it in a prominent place. Make a real effort to learn the verse and its "address" (reference of where it is found in the Bible).

Second Day: Read Hebrews 5, concentrating on verses 1-4.

1. a. The writer of Hebrews now lays out the qualities required for the Hebrew high priests when the office was established in the Old Testament. How was the high priest related to those he served? (Hebrews 5:1a)

   b. What was the responsibility of the high priest of Israel? (Hebrews 5:1b)

2. a. In what way was the high priest of Israel able to deal with those who sin? (Hebrews 5:2a)

   b. Why was he able to do this? (Hebrews 5:2b)

3. Because of this, for whom did the high priest of Israel need to offer sacrifices? (Hebrews 5:3)

4. a. How did the high priest of Israel receive this office? (Hebrews 5:4)

   b. Challenge: Read Exodus 28:1-3,29,38; 29:29. How and by whom was the first high priest called to his office, and who would hold the office after him?

c. Challenge: In the following passages, what happened to people who took it upon themselves to perform duties before the Lord to which God had not called them?

Numbers 16:1-40 (summarize briefly)

1 Samuel 13:8-14

2 Chronicles 26:16-20

5. Personal: God set up the high priesthood in the Old Testament to represent His sinful people before Him, and to offer gifts and sacrifices for sin. Even in that day, when it seemed there were many "works" required of the people, it was God's initiative and God's plan that provided salvation for His people. All that was truly required of them was obedience. That is all that He asks from us today, as well—an attitude of humility and obedience. Have there been times when you have tried to take the reins of your life into your own hands? What happened?

Third Day: Review Hebrews 5, concentrating on verses 5-6.

1. a. According to Hebrews 5:5a, what honor didn't Christ take upon Himself?

b. Read John 8:54. How did Jesus' own words confirm this?

c. Review: How does this compare with the appointment of Aaron and his descendants as high priests? (Hebrews 5:4)

2. The writer now cites two passages from the Psalms to back up his portrayal of Christ as our great high priest who was appointed by God. What does he quote in Hebrews 5:5b (from Psalm 2:7), showing that Jesus has rights in Heaven, where He ministers on our behalf?

3. The Old Testament priests offered sacrifices, but those sacrifices could not truly take away sin. They were just symbols of the final, effective sacrifice that Jesus would offer for us. How does Romans 8:3 express this?

4. Each Old Testament priest served in his day and then died, and a new priest would take his place. What does the writer quote in Hebrews 5:6 (from Psalm 110:4) that shows how Jesus' priesthood is different?

5. a. Challenge: Read Genesis 14, which tells of Melchizedek. How was Abram's (Abraham's) response to Melchizedek king of Salem (verses 18-20) different from his response to the king of Sodom (verses 21-24)? Why do you think he responded this way?

    b. Challenge: In Scripture, there was no succession of priests from Melchizedek. How was this unlike the Aaronic priesthood, and how is Jesus' priesthood like this?

6. Personal: Jesus, the Son of God, willingly took on the responsibility of becoming our high priest forever. He always stands ready to represent you before the Father, to cover your sins with the blood of His sacrifice. Have you allowed Him to do this for you?

Fourth Day: Review Hebrews 5, concentrating on verse 7.

1. a. The writer of Hebrews now moves on to another qualification for the high priesthood that Jesus shared with the high priests of Aaron's line, His membership in humanity. How does he express this in the first phrase of Hebrews 5:7?

    b. Read John 1:14. Was Jesus truly a man, subject to all the weakness and limitations of flesh and blood?

2. a. How is Jesus' experience in the Garden of Gethsemane before His crucifixion related in Hebrews 5:7b?

    b. Challenge: Read Matthew 26:36-46 and Luke 22:39-46. Write down verses or phrases that portray Jesus' human weakness and emotions, and His attitude about what the Father had called Him to do.

3. What does the writer of Hebrews say about the effect of Jesus' prayer during this time? Why was this so? (Hebrews 5:7c)

4. a. Hebrews says that God the Father heard Jesus' prayer. What was Jesus' prayer in the first part of Luke 22:42?

    b. After this prayer, Jesus went to the cross and died for us. What was the second part of His prayer in Luke 22:42 that explains why He did this?

    c. How does Luke 22:43 say that God the Father answered Jesus' prayer?

5. Personal: God does not always answer, "Yes," to our prayers to be delivered from a difficult situation. But when we pray for His will to be done, He will always strengthen us to do His will. What difficult situation are you facing today? Have you been praying to be delivered *from* the situation? Have you considered praying that God will deliver you *through* the situation, according to His will?

Fifth Day: Review Hebrews 5, concentrating on verses 8-10.

1. a. What was Jesus' status according to Hebrews 5:8a? Would you expect a person holding this status to suffer?

    b. Jesus did suffer. What did He learn from this, according to Hebrews 5:8b? Remember that He did not move from disobedience into obedience. Rather, He learned obedience by actually obeying.[1]

    c. Read Hebrews 12:7. Those who accept Jesus as Savior and Lord are children of God. How are we to follow in Jesus' footsteps?

2. a. What characteristic did Jesus' suffering produce in His human nature? (Hebrews 5:9a) Again, this does not mean that Jesus started out imperfect. Rather, it expresses the result of actually suffering, as opposed to merely being willing to suffer.[2]

    b. What was the result of Jesus' suffering, and who benefits from this result? (Hebrews 5:9b)

3. What important thought does Hebrews 5:10 repeat about Jesus?

4. Although Jesus was always without sin, He learned obedience from what He suffered. We, on the other hand, are sinners who have been made perfect by the shed blood of Jesus when we receive Him as Savior and Lord. Although our sins are forgiven, we still have much to learn about obedience as we live day by day. Read 1 John 5:3-4. How are we able to obey God's commands?

---

1. *The Expositor's Bible Commentary*.
2. Ibid.

5. Personal: Do you want to obey God, but sometimes find it hard to do? If you want to, write a prayer here expressing your willingness to do His will, and your need for His help to do it.

Sixth Day: Review Hebrews 5, concentrating on verses 11-14.

1. Why did the writer of Hebrews find it difficult to explain these truths about Christ to his readers? (Hebrews 5:11)

2. a. These readers had apparently been Christians for quite some time. How is their actual progress in the faith compared to what it should be by this time? (Hebrews 5:12)

   b. Challenge: How are all believers to be "teachers," according to the following passages?
   Colossians 3:16

   1 Peter 3:15

3. How does the author explain his reference to spiritual "milk" and "solid food" in Hebrews 5:13-14?

4. a. Where do we obtain spiritual "solid food" according to 2 Timothy 3:16-17?

   b. How does constantly taking in this solid food enable us to distinguish good from evil, according to Philippians 1:9-11?

5. Personal: By doing this Bible study, you are regularly taking in spiritual solid food, equipping yourself to discern good from evil, so that you will be filled with the fruit of righteousness. Have you thanked God for this nourishing food that He has provided? Why not write a prayer about this here?

Hebrews
Lesson 8

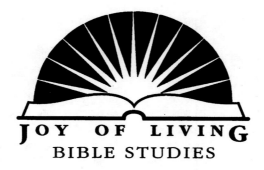

JOY OF LIVING
BIBLE STUDIES

Hebrews 5

We come now in our study to perhaps the most important section of the letter to the Hebrews. It extends through the tenth chapter and presents the vital doctrine of the priesthood of the Lord Jesus Christ. Through the ages people have recognized their wrongdoing, and have known that there must be a God who is offended (see Romans 1:17-20). They have sensed the need for the forgiveness of God. In Israel, before God appointed priests to offer sacrifices, the family head offered sacrifices to God (see Exodus 20:22-24; 28:1). Both of these means of sacrifice became obsolete when Christ came to be our great high priest, greater than and far superior to the best of the Levitical order of priests.[1]

Jesus Christ, Martin Luther said, was "clearly a sacrifice entirely different from that which priests offered, a sacrifice consisting of the blood of bulls and goats. The latter was merely a type [picture] of the former. The cross was the altar on which He, consumed by the fire of the boundless love which burned in His heart, presented the living and holy sacrifice of His body and blood to the Father with fervent intercession, loud cries, and hot anxious tears. That is the true sacrifice. Once and for all it takes away the sins of the world and brings everlasting reconciliation and forgiveness…He must unceasingly represent us before the Father and intercede for us that such weakness and sin may not be reckoned to our account."

As an introduction to the subject of priesthood, the writer of Hebrews defines the qualifications of a high priest in Hebrews 5:1-4. First, his authority must come from God. He could not be self-appointed; rather, God chose him. As we will see in Hebrews 5:5, Jesus, our great high priest, shares this qualification: God the Father appointed Him to this position.

In addition, the high priest must be compassionate and able to empathize with those he represented. If their sins moved him only to anger, he could not intervene before God for them. Israel's priest was one who could pity, who could deal gently with the erring ones, for he knew in his heart his own sin and failure. Like all Israelites, he had experienced the consequences of sin. Daily he had to offer gifts and sacrifices to God on his own behalf, so that he might be purified and accepted by God as one fit to bridge the gap between sinful men and a holy God. In the same way, the Lord Jesus, our great high priest, perfectly understands and sympathizes with us because He walked among us and experienced the trials and temptations we also face (although He never sinned).

The Jewish high priest offered both "gifts and sacrifices for sins" (Hebrews 5:1). The gifts—freewill offerings—were offered to God for His glory. They were brought in recognition of God's goodness and humanity's dependence upon Him. We have nothing except what God gives us; we return it to Him in our gifts. The sacrifices, on the other hand, were offerings to make atonement for sin. The gifts and sacrifices under the Old Testament system are described in Leviticus chapters 1 through 7. These are rich in meaning, revealing God's holiness and mercy. They foreshadow Christ as the Savior of sinners, the perfect Sacrifice.

The Levitical Sacrifices and Offerings

There are instructions for five sacrifices and offerings described in Leviticus 1-7: burnt, grain, fellowship, sin, and guilt. The burnt offering (see Leviticus 1) was unique in that it must be placed on the altar and consumed by fire in its entirety. The believing Israelite saw in this the necessity for complete consecration of the worshiper. His offering was beyond recall. This pictures Christ as He gave all of Himself on the cross.

The grain offering (see Leviticus 2) was distinguished by the absence of shed blood. It consisted of products of the soil. However, it accompanied the burnt offering (see Exodus 29:38-42). The "fine flour" speaks of Christ's flawless character and all that He said or did in the power of the Holy Spirit. The flour was mixed with oil, a symbol of the Holy Spirit. Frankincense, the resin of a particular tree, was included with the handful of the grain offering that was burned on the altar, filling the air with a pungent, pleasurable fragrance. Both the burnt offering and the grain offering were the offerings of individuals. Both are called perpetual offerings because they were offered daily by the priests. The portion of the grain offering that was not burned on the altar became food for the priests.

The fellowship offering (see Leviticus 3; also called a peace or thank offering) expressed the idea of friendship with God made possible by the shedding of blood. Only the animal's fat and kidneys were burned, and its blood was sprinkled against the altar. The priests received a portion of the offering for their food (see Leviticus 7:34), and the remainder became a feast for the worshiper and his family, to be eaten "in the presence of the LORD your God" (see Deuteronomy 12:6-7,17-18). This is a beautiful symbol of what the Lord Jesus Christ has

1. Levitical priests: see footnote page 43.

done in offering Himself for our sins. When we open our lives to Him, He invites us to feast with Him (see Revelation 3:20).

The sin offering (see Leviticus 4:1—5:13) and the guilt offering (see Leviticus 5:14—6:7) were very similar. The purpose of the sin offering was to allow the penitent sinner to receive a full restoration of fellowship with God by offering a sacrifice for general sins, while the purpose of the guilt offering was to deal with sins that inured other people or detracted from the sacred worship. The sin offering emphasized substitutionary atonement by the laying of hands on the offering before it was killed.[1] This portrays Christ putting away sin by the sacrifice of Himself "outside the city gate" (Hebrews 13:11-12). It was for you He died. The apostle Peter wrote, "He himself bore our sins in his body on the tree, so that we might die to sins and live for righteousness; by his wounds you have been healed" (1 Peter 2:24).

Our blessed Lord Jesus, as our great high priest, has offered both gifts and sacrifices for sins. We are awed, yet we rejoice in the perfection of the offering and the Offerer whose declaration on the cross, "It is finished" (John 19:30), was confirmed in His resurrection (see Luke 24).

Christ, Our High Priest

Although the Levitical priesthood functioned in Israel for hundreds of years, it began to deteriorate. Priests failed to observe the laws of the offerings. Some were guilty of keeping for themselves that which God had ordered should be placed on the altar (see 1 Samuel 2:12-17). Later there were instances of men acquiring the office by force, and during the time Rome ruled over Israel, the high priest was appointed by the governing authorities. Assuming the office of priesthood did not make a man God's servant; rather, he must be called by God.

Hebrews 5:5, quoting from Psalm 110:4, confirms that Jesus Christ met this qualification for becoming our great high priest: "So Christ also did not take upon himself the glory of becoming a high priest. But God said to him...'You are a priest for ever, in the order of Melchizedek.'" Melchizedek was king of Salem and "priest of God Most High" (Genesis 14:18). He and Abraham met as Abraham returned from a victorious battle against an allied group of four kings who had defeated another group of five kings and carried off all of their people and goods, including Abraham's nephew Lot and his family. Abraham recovered all the goods and rescued all the captured people. On this occasion, Melchizedek blessed Abraham, and Abraham in turn gave him a tenth of the goods recovered in battle. It is of this priest-king that God spoke in Psalm 110:4, when He designated Christ "high priest in the order of Melchizedek." There was no succession of priests from Melchizedek. Christ's priesthood is of the same kind: He has no successor—His priesthood is eternal.

Although the Lord Jesus never sinned, while He lived on earth as a human being He submitted to all the consequences of sin, such as hunger, thirst, persecution, fatigue, and finally death. He was truly human and He expressed His needs to the Father, as Hebrews 5:7 confirms: "He offered up prayers and petitions with loud cries and tears to

the one who could save him from death." No doubt the pressures of all mankind's guilt weighed heavily on our Lord; His anguish was not restricted to Gethsemane, for He was a "man of sorrows" (see Isaiah 53:3).

Our finite minds and human frailties hinder our comprehension of our Savior's extreme suffering. In His purity, perfection and holiness, He bore the vileness and the wretchedness of all depraved humanity. He wept not because of His mistreatment at the hands of His enemies, but because He was overwhelmed by the weight of all human guilt and the horror of God's anger against sin. Christ prayed to be sustained, for it was as a man that He went to the cross. God granted the needed strength, and delivered His Son through death to His triumphant resurrection. Christ's victory in all His distresses and sufferings is a pledge and assurance that in all that we face, we too are more than conquerors through Him (see Romans 8:37).

At first reading, the next verse—"Although he was a son, he learned obedience from what he suffered" (Hebrews 5:8)—might seem to be inconsistent with the view of Christ's perfection and excellence set forth in the earlier chapters of Hebrews. The phrase "although He was a son" refers back to Hebrews 5:5, where the quote from Psalm 2:7 reminds us that because Jesus was God's Son, He possessed all of the qualifications for His office. In becoming man, Christ submitted Himself in obedience to the Father's will, even to death on the cross (see Philippians 2:6-8). That He "learned obedience" doesn't mean that He ever resisted the will of God. In His incarnation, He submitted to His Father's will. It was this constant choosing of God's will that is described as "learning obedience."

In the many experiences of our lives, God speaks to us. When pleasant and good things are ours, we rejoice in God's love, tender care and goodness. Yet He also speaks to us in our trials, urging us to continually depend on His all-sufficient grace and assuring us of His presence and peace. When we refuse to accept what He sends, rebellion makes us deaf to His voice. What is your attitude when your world turns upside down? Are you listening in obedience to what the Lord has to say to you? (See Proverbs 3:11,12; Isaiah 41:10.)

The experiences through which Christ passed served to make Him perfect. He already possessed moral perfection, which was His eternally. The word "perfect" in Hebrews 5:9 refers to something that has perfectly fulfilled the purpose for which it was designed. Every circumstance, every experience, every suffering and trial perfectly fitted Christ to become the Savior. This was particularly seen in His obedience and submission. Luke 9:51 says that as the time of Jesus' suffering and death approached, "He resolutely set out for Jerusalem." His perfecting was accomplished by His offering of Himself, His consecration to the priestly office. By offering Himself as a sacrifice to God, He discharged the function of a priest. Calvin said, "Here is the ultimate end, why it was necessary for Christ to suffer: that He might thus become initiated into the priesthood."

After Jesus was made perfect, Hebrews 5:9 continues, "he became the source of eternal salvation for all who obey him." Salvation consists in being saved from punishment for sins by trusting in the

---

1. *The Expositor's Bible Commentary.*

blood of Christ as the perfect sacrifice. Further, it is being saved from our own will and enabled to do the will of God.

The priesthood of Christ exceeded the Levitical order in every point. Christ is far superior to Aaron. Aaron was a man; Christ is the Son of God. Aaron offered sacrifices continually; Christ's one sacrifice was sufficient. Aaron brought sacrifices for his own sins; Christ is sinless. Aaron's sacrifices were from flocks and herds; Christ gave Himself. The sacrifices of Aaron were continuous, and only temporary atonement was achieved. Christ's salvation is eternal. Aaron offered sacrifices for Israel. Christ's sacrifice is for all who choose to put their trust in Him (see John 3:16). In Isaiah 1:18 we read, "'Come now, let us reason together,' says the LORD. 'Though your sins are like scarlet, they shall be as white as snow; though they are red as crimson, they shall be like wool.'" Have you obeyed God's invitation to believe? Have you, by faith, entered into eternal salvation?

Spiritual Milk or Solid Food?

Upon first hearing the gospel, these Hebrews had received it with joy. They had been taught by the apostles and were eager to learn. Now, thirty years after Pentecost, they had become negligent, lazy Christians. The writer exclaims, "We have much to say about this, but it is hard to explain because you are slow to learn. In fact, though by this time you ought to be teachers, you need someone to teach you the elementary truths of God's word all over again. You need milk, not solid food!" (Hebrews 5:11-12). The Hebrews failed to realize that to increase in the knowledge of God requires wholehearted attention to the things of the Lord (see Colossians 1:10). If we do not move forward, we slip backward. Instead of being in a position of usefulness to the Lord, they needed to be re-taught their ABC's.

Believers encounter many snares as we live in this world. We hear worldly wisdom, empty promises, and false voices on every side. We must grow up in the Lord so that we may discern what is good and what is evil. We should know when we read or hear false doctrine. Satan disguises himself as an angel of light (see 2 Corinthians 11:14). Don't let him lull you to sleep in your self-satisfaction. The apostle Peter urged, "But grow in the grace and knowledge of our Lord and Savior Jesus Christ" (2 Peter 3:18; see also Ephesians 4:11-15). How is God calling you to mature in your faith and grow in your knowledge of the Lord Jesus?

Study Questions

Before you begin your study this week:

- ઐ Pray and ask God to speak to you through His Holy Spirit.
- ઐ Use only the Bible for your answers.
- ઐ Write down your answers and the verses you used.
- ઐ Answer the "Challenge" questions if you have the time and want to do them.
- ઐ Share your answers to the "Personal" questions with the class only if you want to share them.

First Day: Read the Commentary on Hebrews 5.

1. What meaningful or new thought did you find in the commentary on Hebrews 5 or from your teacher's lecture? What personal application did you choose to apply to your life?

2. Look for a verse in the lesson to memorize this week. Write it down, carry it with you, or post it in a prominent place. Make a real effort to learn the verse and its "address" (reference of where it is found in the Bible).

Second Day: Read Hebrews 6, concentrating on verses 1-3.

1. a. The writer has just declared that his Hebrew readers are still in need of spiritual "milk," in spite of the time that has passed since they became Christians. What does he urge them to do? (Hebrews 6:1a)

    b. He lists some of the elementary teachings that the Hebrews should not have to be taught all over again. What are the first two things required of a believer? (Hebrews 6:1b)

    c. How does Paul's message in Acts 20:21 confirm this foundational truth?

2. What other areas of instruction did the writer say should not have to be repeated to the Hebrews? (Hebrews 6:2)

3. a. We are not certain what the writer of Hebrews meant when he referred to "baptisms" (plural). What do you learn about baptism from 1 Corinthians 12:13?

    b. We are baptized into the body of Christ by the Holy Spirit; however, all Christians also believe in the importance of water baptism as a symbol of our link to Jesus, who was Himself baptized in the Jordan River. (See Matthew 3:13-17. There are different beliefs on the manner of water baptism which we will not address.) How important do you think water baptism is, based on the following verses?

        Matthew 28:19

        Acts 8:12

c. Challenge: As we have noted, the word translated "baptisms" is plural, which is unusual in reference to Christian baptism.[1] The same word is used in Mark 7:4 and Hebrews 9:10. From these verses, what might the writer of Hebrews be referring to in Hebrews 6:2?

4. a. Challenge: "The laying on of hands" was practiced for a number of different reasons in the early church. Read the following Scripture passages and briefly describe what was happening in each situation and why they were "laying on hands".

Acts 13:2-3

Acts 28:7-8

b. Challenge: What do you learn about the last two "elementary" areas of instruction, "the resurrection of the dead, and eternal judgment," from John 5:26-29 and Revelation 20:11-13?

5. a. The writer urges the Hebrews to move on with him to spiritual maturity, but what does he acknowledge is necessary for this plan to succeed? (Hebrews 6:3)

b. Why is this attitude necessary and right, according to James 4:13-15?

6. Personal: What is your attitude toward plans that you make, even plans that are for godly purposes? If you have tended to ignore God's sovereignty over your life, why not pray now and ask Him to continually remind you of your dependence on and responsibility to Him?

Third Day: Review Hebrews 6, concentrating on verses 4-8.

1. What extremely serious warning does the writer give in Hebrews 6:4-6?

2. The people the writer is depicting are those who have been numbered among the followers of Christ, but now leave that company.[2] While some commentators believe the writer is referring to genuine Christians who fall away, that viewpoint seems to contradict what Jesus Himself said. According to John 6:37 and 10:27-29, how is a Christian able to persevere in faith—by the power of God, or by human effort?

---

1. *The Expositor's Bible Commentary*.
2. Ibid.

3. Challenge: It appears that Hebrews 6:4-6 may be speaking of a person whose commitment to Christ seems real to human observers, but something is lacking, and he or she does not truly know the Lord. How did Jesus illustrate this in Mark 4:3-8,16-19?

4. What additional warning is given in Hebrews 6:7-8? What specifically gives the land the ability to produce a useful crop?

5. Read Galatians 5:19-23. What determines the type of fruit that a person's life will produce?

6. Personal: The writer of Hebrews has warned his readers that they must mature in their faith. If they truly belong to the Lord Jesus Christ, He will not allow them to fall away. But they seem to be stalled in an immature state, and are not yet bearing the fruit that God wants to bring forth in their lives. If you are a Christian, are you becoming mature in Christ? Is your life producing a "useful crop" of the Holy Spirit's fruit? Why not pray about this now?

Fourth Day: Review Hebrews 6, concentrating on verses 9-12.

1. The writer of Hebrews has just warned his readers about the danger of producing spiritual thorns and thistles (the fruit of the sinful nature) instead of a useful crop (the fruit of the Spirit). What encouragement does he now offer them in Hebrews 6:9?

2. a. What attributes of God's character allow the writer to have confidence that his readers will persevere in their faith? (Hebrews 6:10)

   b. Hebrews 6:10 is not saying that these believers were saved by their works. Rather, it is saying that after they turned to Christ in faith, their changed lives showed evidence of that faith. Read 1 John 4:19-21. How were the Hebrew believers able to fulfill God's command to love and help others?

3. a. How does the writer again urge perseverance in Hebrews 6:11, and for what purpose?

b.   Challenge: Read 2 Peter 1:5-11. How does Peter make the same point?

4.   Whose example are the Hebrew believers to follow? (Hebrews 6:12)

5.   Personal: The Bible is full of examples of people who persevered in their faith. (A partial list is given in Hebrews 11.) We can also follow the example of men and women of faith that we know personally, or of whom we hear or read. Whose example are you following in your spiritual life? Would you like to learn more about Christians throughout history, perhaps through biographies, movies, or other media?

Fifth Day: Review Hebrews 6, concentrating on verses 13-17.

1.   a.   The author of Hebrews has just urged his readers "to imitate those who through faith and patience inherit what has been promised" (Hebrews 6:12). Whom does he cite as an example, and what did God promise this person? (Hebrews 6:13-14)

b.   Challenge: Read the original accounts to see God's full promise to Abraham in Genesis 12:1-3, and His repetition of the promise with an oath in Genesis 22:15-18. Write down your thoughts about this.

2.   a.   Did Abraham receive what God promised? (Hebrews 6:15)

b.   Challenge: The complete fulfillment of God's promise could not take place within Abraham's lifetime, but he did see a partial fulfillment of the promise. Compare Genesis 12:1-4; 21:5; 25:7-8,24-26. How many years after God first made the promise did Abraham have to wait until his son Isaac was born? How many more years passed before his grandsons through Isaac were born?

3.   Why does a man or woman swear an oath? (Hebrews 6:16).

4.   Though God had no need to swear an oath (there is no one greater than Himself), why did He do it? (Hebrews 6:17)

5. Hebrews 6:17 says God's oath confirmed His promise not only to Abraham but also "to the heirs of what was promised." Who are these heirs according to Galatians 3:29?

6. Personal: If you are a believer in Jesus Christ, you are one of the heirs to God's promise to Abraham. God told Abraham, "I will bless you…and you will be a blessing. I will bless those who bless you…and all peoples on earth will be blessed through you" (Genesis 12:2-3). How has God already fulfilled this promise to you, and what do you think He will do in the future?

Sixth Day: Review Hebrews 6, concentrating on verses 18-20.

1. God's promise and His confirming oath are the "two unchangeable things" in Hebrews 6:18.[1] What does this do for every believer that might otherwise despair in this sinful world? (Hebrews 6:18)

2. a. How is this hope from God illustrated in Hebrews 6:19a?

   b. How did the psalmist express this same thought in Psalm 62:5-6?

3. a. Where does this hope from God enter? (Hebrews 6:19b)

   b. The "inner sanctuary" was the "Most Holy Place" of the tabernacle (and later, of the temple). Leviticus 16 gives instructions for the annual sin offering on the Day of Atonement. Only the high priest was allowed to enter the Most Holy Place, and even he could enter only one time each year. Why was entry into the Most Holy Place so restricted? (Leviticus 16:2)

   c. What did the high priest do when he entered the Most Holy Place each year? (Leviticus 16:15)

4. a. Why is our hope from God able to enter "the inner sanctuary behind the curtain"? (Hebrews 6:20)

   b. Jesus made it possible for us to enter into God's presence "behind the curtain" by atoning for us with His own blood. How was this confirmed when He died on the cross, according to Matthew 27:50-51?

5. Personal: Have you taken hold of the hope God offers, by accepting Jesus' sacrifice for your sin? Do you realize that this is what allows you the privilege of entering the presence of God? In what ways do you find that this hope is "an anchor for [your] soul, firm and secure"?

---

1. *The Expositor's Bible Commentary*.

Hebrews
Lesson 9

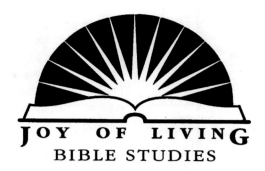

JOY OF LIVING
BIBLE STUDIES

Hebrews 6

A student who had chosen his college major later lamented that it seemed to him that each time he registered for a continuing class the course was labeled an "introduction" to further study on the subject! He felt he would never get finished at this rate. A builder would never finish his project if he kept pouring more foundation and neglected to add the superstructure. Foundations are vital but they are not the whole house. A foundation with a roof added provides some shelter in a storm, but certainly will not provide the comforts of a completed home. So it is in a Christian life. The writer of Hebrews opens chapter 6 by urging believers to build on the great foundation truths of the Christian faith, in order to avoid the tragedy of arrested development in maturity.

There are Christians whose faith has apparently experienced no development in five, ten, or forty years. Still spiritual "babies," they continue to be satisfied with spiritual milk. They have neglected opportunities to be taught in the Word and to grow in the knowledge of their Savior. Such immature believers may never have grown up in behavior. They lose their tempers; their tongues are untamed; they must have their way; they sulk. Childish conduct is a mark of the immature Christian. To refuse to grow up in the faith is certain to result in great spiritual losses.

The writer to the Hebrews says that Christians must "go on to maturity" (Hebrews 6:1). This, of course, does not imply complete knowledge or complete perfection. It means that we must become more familiar with God's plan and purpose, and therefore be able to discuss what the Bible teaches. We should be able to speak to others about spiritual matters as the Lord gives us opportunities. As we mature, we will reflect more and more the likeness of the Lord Jesus, through the work of the Holy Spirit within us. Hebrews 6 is a plea to press on to completeness. In the first few verses, the writer shows what steps must be taken to achieve growth.

Basic Truths

The author does not intend to repeat the basic truths the Hebrews already knew. While he does not suggest abandoning these elementary teachings, he sees no need to continually lay the foundation. Before he returns to the doctrine of Christ's priesthood, he lists six things considered to be basic to the Christian faith.

1. "The foundation of repentance from acts that lead to death" (Hebrews 6:1). The first step for every believer is to turn to God in repentance after we realize our sin (see Acts 20:21; Romans 3:23).

2. "Faith in God" (Hebrews 6:1). Faith must accompany repentance. Our salvation comes through faith in Christ's substitutionary death on the cross (see Ephesians 1:7-8). There is nothing we can do to earn salvation. Obedience to the law or good works have no merit. We cannot make ourselves righteous (see Ephesians 2:8-9).

3. "Baptisms" (Hebrews 6:2). The word translated "baptisms" is plural, which is unusual in reference to Christian baptism. The same word is used in Mark 7:4 and Hebrews 9:10, referring to washings for purification which were common in Jewish ceremonies. The Jews had many washings and baptisms, so the Christian Jew must come to differentiate the one Christian baptism from the many Jewish ceremonial purification requirements (see Ephesians 4:5).

4. "The laying on of hands" (Hebrews 6:2) was practiced in a number of different ways in the early church. Always accompanied by prayer and sometimes by fasting, believers laid their hands upon other believers for healing, and for dedication to ministry and special service (see Acts 6:1-6; 13:2-3; 28:7-8; 2 Timothy 1:6).

5. "The resurrection of the dead" (Hebrews 6:2). Death is not the end of everything: all people, both believers and unbelievers, will rise from the dead at the end of time. (See John 5:26-29; Revelation 20:11-13.)

6. "Eternal judgment" (Hebrews 6:2). After all people rise from the dead, we will give an account of ourselves to God (see 2 Corinthians 5:10). Those who reject Christ and are thus still in their sins will be condemned to "the second death" (Revelation 20:14-15; see also John 5:29). The wonder of God's grace is that He has punished sin in the death of His Son, and eternal life is available to all who will come to God through Him (see John 3:16-18). What is your choice: eternal judgment or eternal life?

When Christians are content with only the elementary truths of the faith, not wanting to know more, they cannot be the mature Christians God wants them to be. Their discernment, their worship, their knowledge, their service are limited. With determination, the author of Hebrews concludes, "Therefore let us leave the elementary teachings about Christ and go on to maturity...And God permitting, we will do so" (Hebrews 6:1,3). Notice the qualifier, "And God permitting..." Apart from the Holy Spirit's working in us there can be no spiritual advance. Notice that the author includes himself, *"We* will do so" (italics added), for no one ever can exhaust the treasury of the Lord!

Warning Concerning Apostasy

Hebrews 6:4-6 contains a most solemn warning. It speaks of a particular group of people who were favored with more than just a casual acquaintance with the gospel message and the blessings of the Christian faith. However, they had not profited by their opportunities; rather, they had brought shame on the cause of Christ.

The people the writer is depicting are those who have been numbered among the followers of Christ, but now leave that company.[1] While some commentators believe the writer is referring to genuine Christians who fall away, that viewpoint seems to contradict what Jesus Himself said: "My sheep listen to my voice; I know them, and they follow me. I give them eternal life, and they shall never perish; *no one can snatch them out of my hand*. My Father, who has given them to me, is greater than all; *no one can snatch them out of my Father's hand*" (John 10:27-29, italics added). It appears that Hebrews 6:4-6 may be speaking of a person whose commitment to Christ seems real to human observers, but something is lacking, and he or she does not truly know the Lord.

The author gives us a list of things these people had experienced. They had "been enlightened," had "tasted the heavenly gift," had "shared in the Holy Spirit," had "tasted the goodness of the word of God," and finally, had tasted "the powers of the coming age" (Hebrews 6:4-5). This list seems to indicate personal experience and not just hearsay. These people were like those Jesus referred to in His parable of the sower in Mark 4:16-17, "Others, like seed sown on rocky places, hear the word and at once receive it with joy. But since they have no root, they last only a short time. When trouble or persecution comes because of the word, they quickly fall away."

The writer continues, "It is impossible for those…if they fall away, to be brought back to repentance" (Hebrews 6:4,6). Notice that the writer does not say that these people "cannot be forgiven" or "cannot be restored to salvation." Rather, they cannot "be brought back to repentance." After falling into this backsliding, they cannot bring themselves to repent and turn away from their sin once again.

They had been enlightened and stirred by the gospel message. Then they apparently totally abandoned and renounced the basic truths of Christianity. Furthermore, "to their loss they are crucifying the Son of God all over again and subjecting him to public disgrace" (Hebrews 6:6).

The author of Hebrews now illustrates this process from agriculture, "Land that drinks in the rain often falling on it and that produces a crop useful to those for whom it is farmed receives the blessing of God. But land that produces thorns and thistles is worthless and is in danger of being cursed. In the end it will be burned" (Hebrews 6:7-8). Jesus illustrated a similar spiritual truth in Mark 4:18-19, "Still others,

like seed sown among thorns, hear the word; but the worries of this life, the deceitfulness of wealth and the desires for other things come in and choke the word, making it unfruitful." In Jesus' parable, it was the ground—the response of the person—that made the difference. The seed in each case was the same, the Word of God. Likewise, in Hebrews 6:7-8, the people who had "fallen away" had been satisfied to drink in the rain of God's blessings that were available to all. They had some experience in hearing the Word and had seen evidence of the Holy Spirit's working, yet they produced no useful crop, only weeds fit for burning. What a warning for professing Christians whose lives produce only the equivalent of weeds. Which sort of ground are you?

Let Your Light Shine

The author's words in the early verses of Hebrews 6 had probably shocked some of his readers. He would rather scare them with warnings than run the risk of their settling into apathy, neglect, or outright rejection of faith in Christ. He is quick to assure them of his love for them, and his confidence that they had remained faithful. Perhaps his warnings would shake them out of their lethargy and prepare them to move on to maturity.

Hebrews 6:10, "God is not unjust; he will not forget your work and the love you have shown him as you have helped his people and continue to help them," is not saying that these believers were saved by their works. Rather, it is saying that after they turned to Christ in faith, their changed lives showed evidence of that faith. He had reason to believe they were truly saved because they evidenced love for their brothers and sisters in Christ (see 1 John 3:14). A Christian's "works" should be an outward expression of what the grace of God has done within them, a practical ministry of love for fellow-believers and for all people.

The author's longing for the Hebrews was that they "show this same diligence to the very end, in order to make your hope sure" (Hebrews 6:11). Seeing the fruit of the Holy Spirit produced in our lives fully develops the hope that we have in Christ Jesus. We can learn to walk with the Spirit by imitating the example of other believers who have persevered in their faith.

God's Sure Promises

The author of Hebrews has just urged his readers "to imitate those who through faith and patience inherit what has been promised" (Hebrews 6:12). He goes on in verse 13 to cite the example of Abraham, the first patriarch of Israel. Though the patriarchs suffered trials and afflictions, they did not deviate from the path of faith in following the Lord. We are to imitate these faithful people. They inherited the promises of God; they entered His promised rest.

God made many promises to Abraham, His servant chosen to be the father of God's special people. In obedience to God, Abraham left Ur and traveled to Canaan (see Genesis 12:1-3). Many years passed before the promise of a son was realized. Then after the offering of Isaac, God renewed His promise that through Abraham's descendants

---

1. *The Expositor's Bible Commentary.*

all peoples on earth would be blessed (see Genesis 22:15-18). The Lord Jesus is the fulfillment of that promise. The promise was confirmed by an oath, making it doubly binding. God was His own witness and guarantor. Now Abraham had the promise of God based on His eternal purpose and His oath, the sign of His great faithfulness. The blessing and oath serve as an illustration of God's faithfulness. He will carry out His purpose, and His promises will never fail. As a believer, you are an heir to those promises (see Galatians 3:29).

Next the writer describes the believer as one who has fled as a refugee to take hold of the hope offered to him. Upon reading these verses, the Hebrew believers would immediately think of the six cities of refuge God had appointed (see Joshua 20:1-9). Under the law anyone who killed a person accidentally and unintentionally could flee to one of these cities for protection from an avenger. In the same way, by faith we flee from the death penalty for our sin to the only refuge, Jesus Christ, our hope in this life and in all eternity.

What a contrast between the cities of refuge under the Old Testament law and the refuge the gospel proclaims. Only unintentional killers were admitted to the cities of refuge, yet Christ invites all people to come to Him. While the refuge cities of Israel provided safety, refugees were virtually prisoners, but Christ sets us free (see John 8:36). The one who entered one of these cities left his possessions and inheritance behind, while those who take refuge in Christ as Savior become heirs with Him of all the riches and glory He shares with His Father (see Romans 8:13-17).

Moving toward the theme he has mentioned previously, the writer of Hebrews continues his word pictures to describe the benefits of God's great promises. "We have this hope as an anchor for the soul, firm and secure. It enters the inner sanctuary behind the curtain, where Jesus, who went before us, has entered on our behalf. He has become a high priest for ever, in the order of Melchizedek" (Hebrews 6:19-20). In the Levitical system, the high priest entered behind the curtain of the Most Holy Place of the tabernacle only once a year as a representative of the people. They were forbidden to follow him. In fact the people waited rather anxiously for him to come out, for the Most Holy Place was where God promised to meet with him. It was an awesome audience with the holy, majestic, living God.

Jesus, "who went before us," has entered into the presence of God the Father in heaven "on our behalf" (Hebrews 6:20), and has opened the way for us because of His death. All He has done is for us. Now we have access to the inner sanctuary, the Most Holy Place of all. Christ's sphere of ministry is in the presence of God; He is there for you, keeping watch over all your interests and concerns (see Hebrews 7:22-25).

Study Questions

Before you begin your study this week:
- ❧ Pray and ask God to speak to you through His Holy Spirit.
- ❧ Use only the Bible for your answers.
- ❧ Write down your answers and the verses you used.
- ❧ Answer the "Challenge" questions if you have the time and want to do them.
- ❧ Share your answers to the "Personal" questions with the class only if you want to share them.

First Day: Read the Commentary on Hebrews 6.

1. What meaningful or new thought did you find in the commentary on Hebrews 6 or from your teacher's lecture? What personal application did you choose to apply to your life?

2. Look for a verse in the lesson to memorize this week. Write it down, carry it with you, or post it in a prominent place. Make a real effort to learn the verse and its "address" (reference of where it is found in the Bible).

Second Day: Read Hebrews 7:1-22, concentrating on verses 1-3.

1. a. Hebrews chapter 6 ended with the words, "Jesus…has become a high priest forever, in the order of Melchizedek." This was previously mentioned in chapter 5, and we looked briefly at Melchizedek's story (from Genesis 14) at that time. Now the author of Hebrews develops this theme in more detail. Who was Melchizedek? (Hebrews 7:1a)

   b. What did Melchizedek do for Abraham? (Hebrews 7:1b)

   c. What did Abraham give Melchizedek? (Hebrews 7:2a)

2. a. What are the meanings of Melchizedek's name and title? (Hebrews 7:2b)

   b. Challenge: According to the following verses, how do Melchizedek's name and title point to two distinctive aspects of Christ's saving work?

   Romans 3:21-24

Romans 5:1-2

3. What facts about Melchizedek does Scripture not record? (Hebrews 7:3a)

4. What significant truth about Jesus Christ does the record of Melchizedek point to? (Hebrews 7:3b)

5. If you read through the book of Genesis, the few verses about Melchizedek in chapter 14 might seem rather unimportant, like a footnote to Abraham's story. Yet as we see from this section of the book of Hebrews, those few verses in Genesis 14 have great significance. What do the following verses say about the inspiration and power of the Bible?

   Mark 12:24

   Romans 15:4

   2 Peter 1:20-21

   2 Timothy 3:14-17

6. Personal: What is your attitude about the Bible? Do you desire to really *know* God's Word, as Jesus said in Mark 12:24, so that you will not "be in error"?

Third Day: Review Hebrews 7:1-22, concentrating on verses 4-10.

1. In the author's time, it was generally recognized that there was an obligation to pay tithes to important religious functionaries. The ones who paid were in some way subject to those to whom the tithe was paid.[1] How does Hebrews 7:4 say the greatness of Melchizedek was proved?

---

1. *The Expositor's Bible Commentary*.

2. a. According to the law of Moses, who was required to pay a tithe and who received it? (Hebrews 7:5)

   b. Challenge: Read Numbers 18:21,26,28. How does this support Hebrews 7:5?

   c. How did Abraham's tithe, paid to Melchizedek, contrast with the tithing system set up in the law of Moses? (Hebrews 7:6a)

3. What else did Melchizedek do in relation to Abraham, and what did this mean? (Hebrews 7:6b-7)

4. What characteristic is declared about Melchizedek in Hebrews 7:8b? How does this contrast with those who receive tithes under the law of Moses in Hebrews 7:8a?

5. What further argument is made in Hebrews 7:9-10 that shows the superiority of the priesthood of Melchizedek over the Levitical priesthood?

6. a. You may wonder why the author spends so much time proving Melchizedek's superiority over the Levitical priesthood. Why does it matter? Look back at Hebrews 7:3b for the answer.

   b. Personal: The author used Melchizedek as an illustration to be sure his readers understood that Jesus Christ is superior to the Levitical priests—the most important people in his readers' religious background and culture. Jesus offered the answer to the problem the Levitical priests could not solve. Who does your culture say has the answers to life's problems—Movie stars? Political figures? Business leaders? Spiritual teachers? How would you explain to someone you know that Jesus offers a better or superior answer than these people?

Fourth Day: Review Hebrews 7:1-22, concentrating on verses 11-14.

1. a. What does the first phrase of the author's question in Hebrews 7:11 imply about the ability of the law and the Levitical priesthood to make anyone perfect (acceptable to God)?

   b. How does Romans 8:3a confirm this?

2. What did the failure of the Levitical priesthood (Aaron's line) point to the need for? (Hebrews 7:11b)

3. a. Since the Levitical priesthood was set up by the law of Moses, what must change when the Levitical priesthood fails? (Hebrews 7:12)

    b. Read Romans 8:2. What change of law came about in Jesus Christ?

4. What tribe of Israel was Jesus from? Did that tribe have anything to do with the priesthood under the law of Moses? (Hebrews 7:13-14)

5. Personal: Many people try to live by the Ten Commandments, or by some set of rules that they think will make them acceptable to God. But, as we have seen in Romans 8:3, living by the law or a set of rules cannot make us acceptable to God because we are operating out of our sinful nature. This dooms us from the start; we can never be perfect. When Jesus Christ came, He brought a change of the law—"the law of the Spirit of life" (Romans 8:2). Have you accepted His priestly sacrifice of Himself so that you may have life? If you have, write down what this means to you.

Fifth Day: Review Hebrews 7:1-22, concentrating on verses 15-19.

1. What aspect of Christ's superiority does the author point out in Hebrews 7:15-16?

2. What do you learn about this characteristic of Jesus' life in the following verses?

    John 5:26

    Acts 2:23-24

    Revelation 1:18

3. What testimony to this fact does the author again cite from Scripture? (Hebrews 7:17, quoting Psalm 110:4)

4. a. Why was the Levitical system set aside at the coming of Christ? (Hebrews 7:18-19a)

    b. What can we do through Jesus Christ that we could never do under the law? (Hebrews 7:19b)

5. a. How does Acts 13:39 confirm the message of Hebrews 7:18-19?

    b. Read Romans 5:1-2. What "better hope" results from our justification by faith in Jesus Christ?

6. Personal: Just think—Jesus offers the power of His "indestructible life" to you! Have you accepted the eternal life that He offers? Write out John 3:16-17, inserting your name.

Sixth Day: Review Hebrews 7:1-22, concentrating on verses 20-22.

1. What certified the permanence and security of the priesthood of Jesus Christ? (Hebrews 7:20-21)

2. What has Jesus become? (Hebrews 7:22)

3. Read Luke 22:14-20. How did Jesus describe the new and better covenant to his apostles?

4. a. Challenge: Hebrews 7:21 emphasized that God's oath meant that He would not change His mind. His new covenant would be established according to His will. Read Luke 22:39-44. Was it easy for Jesus to carry out the Father's will in establishing the new covenant? (Luke 22:44)

    b. Challenge: In spite of His natural human feelings about what He had to do, what was Jesus' attitude towards His Father's will? (Luke 22:42)

5. Personal: Jesus was the willing guarantee of a better covenant. He was willing to suffer death on the cross, and even worse, to experience complete separation from God the Father as He paid for humanity's sin. How does this make you feel? Write a prayer expressing what this means to you.

Hebrews
Lesson 10

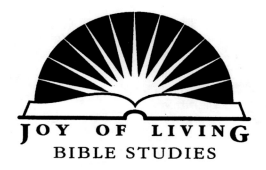

JOY OF LIVING
BIBLE STUDIES

Hebrews 7:1-22

Three times the author has introduced that strange designation from Psalm 110:4, "a priest...in the order of Melchizedek," in Hebrews 5:6 and 10 and Hebrews 6:20. In Hebrews 5:11 the writer indicates that this topic will be hard to explain since his readers "are slow to learn." They have now been prepared in Hebrews 5:12—6:20 by his warning, his counsel to go on to maturity, and his assurance of God's eternal purpose and His faithfulness. Hebrews 7 is a sermon based on Psalm 110:4: "The LORD has sworn and will not change his mind: 'You are a priest for ever, in the order of Melchizedek.'"

Who is this Melchizedek? Except for the reference in Psalm 110 and the first mention of him in Genesis 14:18, we are left in the dark about him. Some have thought he was an angel or the Holy Spirit. Some Jewish writers think he was Shem, Noah's son, but there is no account of his living in Canaan, and it is not likely he would have changed his name. Some Christian writers suggest that Melchizedek was a theophany, an appearance of Christ prior to His incarnation. This view would make Christ a "type" or "picture" of Himself, an unusual circumstance. The generally accepted opinion is that he was a king who reigned in Salem, later called Jerusalem. He worshiped God; he was a priest; and he was a type of Christ. God has revealed enough about this king-priest to arouse our curiosity so that we will dig deeper to uncover all that may elude those who skim the surface.

Why, do you suppose, did the writer choose Melchizedek to show Christ's superiority? It is not only interesting but also amazingly significant that God had a priesthood four hundred years before He established Aaron and his sons in a priestly order. Hebrews 7 shows the superior quality of Melchizedek's priesthood and the features that made it different. It was an entirely new doctrine to assert that Christ was and is forever a high priest. No reference had been made to His priestly office during His earthly ministry. Jewish people who were well-schooled in their history might have objected that Christ did not belong to the Levitical tribe. Hebrews 7 presents evidence that the priesthood of Christ, which was according to the ancient order of Melchizedek, was far more glorious than Aaron's. It is a wonderful thought that Jesus is king as well as priest. He has all authority and universal sovereignty to engage in priestly work on our behalf. He "has gone into heaven and is at God's right hand—with angels, authorities and powers in submission to him" (1 Peter 3:22).

Melchizedek's place in sacred history lends credence to the doctrine of the inspiration of the Scriptures. All we know of him in Genesis is recorded in three short verses. A thousand years pass before the prophetic verse in Psalm 110 was written in which God declared to His son, "You are a priest for ever, in the order of Melchizedek." Another thousand years later that verse became the text for the unfolding of the truths of redemption as revealed in Christ. We can see the hand of God in bringing together Melchizedek and Abraham with a view to Christ's coming. Even the bread and wine they shared were symbols of His priestly office.

What is said of Melchizedek shows how he represented the Lord Jesus in type. Melchizedek was a king; he was king of righteousness and peace. He was priest of God Most High. Melchizedek's genealogy is not given; his priesthood did not descend to him from another, nor was it given to another. He brought bread and wine to refresh Abraham, giving as a king, blessing as a priest. Melchizedek received a tithe, a tenth of everything, from Abraham, as an expression of Abraham's gratitude and as homage to this extraordinary person. The offering may also be viewed as dedicated to God, presented to Him by His appointed priest. Melchizedek was like the Son of God in that his authority was God-given and unique; it was perpetual and went beyond the bounds of Levitical limitations.

Our Lord Jesus, of whom Melchizedek is a picture, is a king of God's anointing, a righteous king. He is the Lord, our righteousness (see 1 Corinthians 1:30). The fruit of righteousness is peace; Christ gives peace and is our peacemaker (see Romans 5:1). The Lord Jesus is priest of God Most High. Jew and Gentile alike must come to God by Him (see John 14:6). Only through Him can we be reconciled to God and receive forgiveness. As in the case of Melchizedek, the priestly office of Christ did not descend from another, nor was it passed on to another. It is His by appointment and is everlasting. As a man, the Lord Jesus had no father; as God, He had no mother. The offering of refreshment reminds us of the goodness and loving kindness of our Lord. He never fails us in our spiritual conflicts; He renews our strength from day to day. He gives a crown of beauty instead of ashes, the oil of gladness to comfort our mourning, and a song of praise to gladden a heavy heart (see Isaiah 61:3).

Our thankfulness to the Lord Jesus for all He has done for us may find expression in several ways. A tithe was the Lord's portion under the law of Moses (see Leviticus 27:30). It proved to be a workable system; the entire tribe of Levi was thus supported, and we never read that they lacked provision. It would seem that in gratitude for the unsearchable riches of Christ, our hearts would desire a substantial portion to be returned to Him. Paul directed the Corinthians to lay aside a sum for the Lord's work in proportion to their earnings (see 1 Corinthians 16:2). Returning to the Lord a portion of what we have received is not limited to money, although that is important and necessary. Each one should seek the Lord's guidance as to how to use all He has entrusted to us, including our time and talents. All of this, of course, follows our having first given ourselves to the Lord (see Romans 12:1; 2 Corinthians 8:5).

Note that Hebrews 7:3 says that Melchizedek was like the Son of God, not vice versa. In point of time Christ existed before Melchizedek, although from a human viewpoint, Melchizedek was a priest before Christ was. The priesthood of the Lord Jesus was ordained and established in the eternal counsels of the God Most High long before Melchizedek came on the scene. However, Melchizedek certainly represented Christ in his office as a priest-king; he is a type of the One who surpasses all others in His perfection and glory. Christ had neither beginning of days nor end of life. His death on the cross affected His humanity; but as God He experienced no interruption of His endless life. He remains a priest forever.

A Priest and a Patriarch

In Luke 24, we read that two disciples were walking along the road to Emmaus the evening of Christ's resurrection. A stranger joined them who knew more than they had learned about the Messiah and the Scriptures. The travelers lamented over the crucifixion of Christ and shared their bewilderment over the story that His body had disappeared. Then the stranger began at Moses and the prophets to expound the Scriptures with clear and revealing explanations. Do you suppose the Holy Spirit has recorded in Hebrews the truths that Christ taught these two disciples? We are better equipped today than Old Testament people were to unravel some of the mysteries of the Old Testament, for they are revealed in and through the Lord Jesus Christ. The timeworn couplet says it well: "The New is in the Old contained; the Old is in the New explained. The New is in the Old concealed; the Old is by the New revealed." Melchizedek is a good illustration of this principle. The references to him in Genesis 14 and Psalm 110 provide little information about him, but in the light of the New Testament, he appears as a type of Christ.

In Hebrews 7:4 the author calls upon his readers to think about this Melchizedek and how great he must have been. None other than Abraham, the one chosen of God to be the founder and head of Israel, recognized Melchizedek as superior. The writer reasons that giving tithes to a servant of God showed respect for his official capacity. Furthermore, there was a high value placed on gifts given by one of such stature and dignity as Abraham. In addition to his headship as Israel's physical father, spiritually he was the "father" of all believers (see Romans 4:16). How great Melchizedek must have been for Abraham to acknowledge his superiority. Since Abraham trusted God, he surely did not act on impulse, but knew Melchizedek as a true priest of God.

So, even though Abraham was a great man and was the one who first received the promise of the covenant, Melchizedek was still greater.

God gave instructions for the Levites to be given tithes by His people. Hebrews 7:5 refers to the sons of Aaron who received tithes as priests. Numbers 18:26-28 explains that the people of Israel brought tithes to the Levites, who then set aside a tenth part for those engaged in the actual duties of the priesthood. The priests, descendants of Aaron, were commanded by the law to receive tithes. Melchizedek, on the other hand, was under no law. He was a king as well as priest of God Most High, and thus was honored by Abraham. The writer of Hebrews stresses the importance and dignity of Abraham to emphasize the high rank of Melchizedek, who pronounced a blessing on Abraham. To summarize his argument the author concludes that there is no question about it—"the lesser person is blessed by the greater" (Hebrews 7:7).

The logic of Hebrews 7:9-10—that Levi, ancestor of the Levitical priesthood, was included with Abraham in paying the tithe to Melchizedek—was understood by the Hebrews. This principle is applied in other instances and should be understood, since corporate representation is the basis for God's dealings with the human race. Adam, for example, represented all people. Consequently, his sin and death are imputed to every man, woman and child: "Sin entered the world through one man, and death through sin, and in this way death came to all men, because all sinned" (Romans 5:12). Likewise, when Christ met the demands of the law, died and rose again, He acted for all who believe on Him. In effect, every believer died with Him and lives in the power of His resurrection. Scripture says, "For if, by the trespass of the one man, death reigned through that one man, how much more will those who receive God's abundant provision of grace and of the gift of righteousness reign in life through the one man, Jesus Christ" (Romans 5:17); "I have been crucified with Christ" (Galatians 2:20); "God...made us alive with Christ...And God raised us up with Christ" (Ephesians 2:4-6). It follows that what Abraham did or received was on behalf of his descendants. God's covenant with him was also with them. God's promises were to Abraham and to his "offspring" (see Genesis 12:7; 13:15), and several hundred years later they entered the Promised Land.

What Need for Change?

When Adam and Eve were created, it was God's plan that they fellowship with Him. Many failures and many years later, God designed another way for Israel to establish a relationship with Him and gain access into His presence. The law told them what they must do to enjoy God's fellowship. Obedience was a requisite for all who would be friends of God. But it was impossible for sinful humans to walk in perfect obedience. The sacrificial system was instituted so that the breach might be healed. The sacrifice was accepted by God as an atonement; it was a covering for sin. It may have provided a sense of well-being, but the conscience of the worshiper could not be cleansed. People could not approach God without fear of judgment.

So while the priesthood and the law were inseparable, neither could take away sin; neither gave personal access and fellowship with God, neither brought lasting peace. It was obvious that the Aaronic priesthood was inadequate. God planned it that way, so that in His perfect wisdom and in His own time He might provide the ultimate solution for the comfort and joy of His redeemed. You see, the Jewish system had to do with rituals, with the altar, incense, animal sacrifice, a temple—all physical things. Sin is a spiritual matter; no earthly priest is able to remove it. "But God demonstrates his own love for us in this: While we were still sinners, Christ died for us" (Romans 5:8). God forgives sin on the basis of faith in the shed blood of the Lord Jesus Christ. Have you put your trust in Him alone?

God had intimated that another priest of a different order would replace the sons of Aaron. This priest was not a Levite but was of the royal tribe of Judah. He was designated a priest forever after the order of king Melchizedek. This newer, higher order brought the perfection lacking in the administration of Aaron and his sons. Perfection means bringing a thing to completeness of purpose or design. Thus the relationship between God and humanity was perfected. Christ has brought us into the presence of God. We may draw near to Him, know Him and fellowship with Him.

Changing the priesthood necessitated a change in the law. Without the Levitical priesthood, there could be no sacrifice and no form of worship. It follows that the law became useless. This, of course, does not refer to the moral law, the Ten Commandments, which are repeated in the New Testament, with the exception of the fourth. The reference is to the Mosaic system, the law of commandments contained in ordinances, which has been abolished, Christ having nailed it to the cross (see Ephesians 2:15; Colossians 2:14). The law and the gospel could not mix.

Further evidence is given to show the Hebrews that they must not cling to Judaism. The priesthood of Christ according to Melchizedek's order was totally different. The Levitical priesthood was passed from father to son. By contrast, Christ is a priest forever, His priestly work executed in the power of an indestructible life. As noted previously, although He died in His human nature, He was and is alive as the eternal, immortal Son of God. Because the Lord Jesus lives forever as our high priest, He is an all-sufficient advocate and intercessor. He is the only priest God has appointed as the mediator between Himself and humanity (see 1 Timothy 2:5). His priestly work is unique. The Lord Jesus offered Himself a sacrifice for our sins; He was both offerer and offering. He intercedes on our behalf as we travel through this world.

Why did God give His people the law of Moses, a law that was weak and unprofitable and that "made nothing perfect" (Hebrews 7:19)? The law was given to make us conscious of our sin, and to hold us accountable to God (see Romans 3:19-20). So, says Hebrews 7:18-19, God set the former regulation aside and introduced a better hope. From the background of mysteries and shadows of Judaism, the Lord Jesus emerges as the true light that lights the world. In Him God manifested the perfections of His person. Christ is the hope, the One looked for and longed for by prophets and kings.

Believers today cherish that "blessed hope—the glorious appearing of our great God and Savior, Jesus Christ" (Titus 2:13). We have the privilege of drawing near to God, a term echoing the approach of priests to God. We are allowed to draw near by the blood of Christ. Believers have access to the Father; and we are a holy priesthood (see 1 Peter 2:5). The complete realization of the "better hope" and our being made perfect is yet future. Then we shall be in the Father's house, to live in His presence forevermore. Until then, "Let us then approach the throne of grace with confidence, so that we may receive mercy and find grace to help us in our time of need" (Hebrews 4:16).

A Guarantee Forever

In Hebrews 7:20-22, the author reminds his readers again that the Lord Jesus was made a priest by the oath of God. The reason people take oaths is that their word may not be trusted; the oath guarantees that what they have sworn they will do. God never needs to do that; He cannot lie, nor deny Himself. Yet He did confirm this statement by an oath, making it of great importance. This put Christ in a position superior to any who had gone before.

Along with the promise of Christ's changeless and permanent priesthood, there is a covenant superior to the one connected with the Levitical priesthood. That earlier covenant, or agreement, was the law of Moses. Its terms were perfect obedience on Israel's part. God agreed that if they kept their promise, they would be His chosen people, His treasure above all people, a kingdom of priests and a holy nation (see Exodus 19:3-8). The new covenant is based on the perfect sacrifice of the Lord Jesus. The Lord Jesus became the guarantee of the covenant by fulfilling all that God required; He is the guarantee of sins forgiven and of all the benefits of redemption in Christ Jesus. He is the pledge that those who trust Him for salvation will receive sustaining grace that they may live wisely and in obedience to their Lord.

What is your response to all that is yours because Christ is your guarantee? Because of the surpassing excellence of who He is, our obligation to Him is greater. What can we give to Him who left the Father's glory to redeem us, to pay our debt and make us free from the law of sin and death? Our high priest pleads the efficacy of His shed blood as He continually intercedes for us. May we surrender wholeheartedly to Him, walking in loving obedience, so that in all things we might show forth His praise and glory. Our very best can never adequately express our love and thankfulness for God's indescribable gift!

Study Questions

Before you begin your study this week:

- ⋙ Pray and ask God to speak to you through His Holy Spirit.
- ⋙ Use only the Bible for your answers.
- ⋙ Write down your answers and the verses you used.
- ⋙ Answer the "Challenge" questions if you have the time and want to do them.
- ⋙ Share your answers to the "Personal" questions with the class only if you want to share them.

First Day: Read the Commentary on Hebrews 7:1-22.

1. What meaningful or new thought did you find in the commentary on Hebrews 7:1-22 or from your teacher's lecture? What personal application did you choose to apply to your life?

2. Look for a verse in the lesson to memorize this week. Write it down, carry it with you, or post it in a prominent place. Make a real effort to learn the verse and its "address" (reference of where it is found in the Bible).

Second Day: Read Hebrews 7:23—8:13, concentrating on 7:23-25.

1. Why did new priests continually have to be added under the Levitical system? (Hebrews 7:23)

2. In this regard, why is Jesus' priesthood superior to the Levitical priesthood? (Hebrews 7:24)

3. a. Read Isaiah 9:6-7, in which the prophet speaks of the coming Messiah. How does this passage confirm this characteristic of Jesus' priesthood?

   b. How does Romans 6:9 make the same point?

4. a. What is Jesus able to do because of His permanent priesthood? (Hebrews 7:25a)

b. What does Jesus always do for those He has saved? (Hebrews 7:25b)

5. a. Read Mark 16:19. Where did Jesus go when He left the earth after His resurrection?

b. Read 1 John 2:1-2. What does Jesus' presence there accomplish on our behalf?

6. Personal: Every believer appreciates the fact that Jesus died for our sin and rose to give us life. But do you realize that He now sits at the right hand of God the Father, and that His very presence there *is* His intercession for us, bearing witness to His sacrifice on our behalf? Write down what this means to you.

Third Day: Review Hebrews 7:23—8:13, concentrating on 7:26-28.

1. What characteristics does Jesus have that enable him to meet our need? (Hebrews 7:26)

2. Read 2 Corinthians 5:21. Why are these characteristics necessary?

3. How does Jesus stand in contrast to the earthly priests? (Hebrews 7:27)

4. How does the author summarize why Jesus' priesthood is better? (Hebrews 7:28)

5. Personal: The high priests of Aaron's line, appointed under the law, were not perfect. Although they may have served God wholeheartedly, they were still sinners, like every other human being. Think of them: day after day, month after month, year after year, offering sacrifices for their own sin and for the sin of the people. What an amazing thing it must have been for the Hebrews, knowing the long history of the Levitical priests, to realize how utterly different, final, and perfect was Jesus' priesthood and sacrifice! Put yourself in their situation—how would this understanding make you feel?

Fourth Day: Review Hebrews 7:23—8:13, concentrating on 8:1-3.

1. What fact pointedly shows the greatness of our great high priest? (Hebrews 8:1)

2. a. Although He occupies such a high place in heaven, what does Jesus do there? (Hebrews 8:2a)

   b. What is this place in which Jesus serves? (Hebrews 8:2b)

3. In the book of Exodus, God gave very detailed instructions to Moses about the place of worship for the people of Israel. What did He tell Moses about this place in Exodus 25:8-9?

4. What do earthly high priests do that Jesus also had to do as our great high priest? (Hebrews 8:3)

5. Read John 6:51. What did Jesus Himself say was His gift and sacrifice?

6. Personal: Jesus serves as our great high priest in the heavenly sanctuary, having given Himself as the complete and perfect sacrifice for sin, once and for all. The Lord set up the true sanctuary and provided the sacrifice—all we have to do is believe and receive His wonderful gift. Have you received it?

Fifth Day: Review Hebrews 7:23—8:13, concentrating on 8:4-7.

1. Jesus' priesthood is not of this earth. How does the author of Hebrews compare the earthly sanctuary in which the Levitical priests served to the one that is in heaven? What was Moses warned of when he was about to build the earthly sanctuary? (Hebrews 8:4-5)

2. Why is Jesus' ministry better? (Hebrews 8:6-7)

3. a. Challenge: Under the old covenant, people who took it upon themselves to approach the Lord and perform priestly duties to which God had not called them actually died. (See Lesson 7, Second Day, Question 4c for details.) Read Numbers 17:12-13. How did the people feel about approaching the Lord after seeing what had happened?

    b. Challenge: Read Numbers 18:1-5. How did God instruct Aaron the high priest, his sons, and the Levites regarding how to protect the Israelites from His wrath?

4. The author of Hebrews never says that the old covenant was bad. God gave the law for a purpose and it was good. But now, Hebrews says, the new covenant is superior to the old one. Read 2 Corinthians 3:6-11. How does this show that the new covenant, of which Jesus is mediator, is better than the old?

5. Personal: Under the new covenant, through Jesus Christ our Savior, we have the amazing privilege of being constantly in the presence of God through His Spirit within us. Read 2 Corinthians 3:18. Paraphrase this verse, inserting your name, or write down what being under the new covenant means to you.

Sixth Day: Review Hebrews 7:23—8:13, concentrating on 8:8-13.

1. In Hebrews 8:8-12 the author quotes at length from Jeremiah 31:31-34. At the time Jeremiah spoke this prophecy, the northern kingdom of Israel and the southern kingdom of Judah had been separated for a long time. With whom would God make the new covenant? (Hebrews 8:8)

2. Even though God had lovingly rescued His people from Egyptian slavery and made a covenant with them, what happened later? (Hebrews 8:9)

3. a. How did Jeremiah prophesy that the new covenant would be different from the old? (Hebrews 8:10-11)

   b. What makes the blessings listed in Hebrews 8:10-11 possible under the new covenant? (Hebrews 8:12)

4. What does the establishment of the new covenant through Jesus Christ mean about the old covenant under the law of Moses? (Hebrews 8:13)

5. The quotation from Jeremiah says that God would make the new covenant "with the house of Israel" (Hebrews 8:8,10). According to the following verses, who may participate in the new covenant? Is it available to more than just the physical descendants of Abraham?

   Matthew 28:16-20

   Romans 4:16-17

6. Personal: Whether your ancestors are Jews or Gentiles, you are invited to receive by faith the forgiveness that comes through Jesus Christ. Have you done this? If so, the Bible says, God has put His laws in your mind and written them on your heart. He will be your God, and you will be His child. And, most amazing, you will *know* Him. Do you spend time daily developing this relationship through reading God's Word and talking with Him in prayer?

Hebrews
Lesson 11

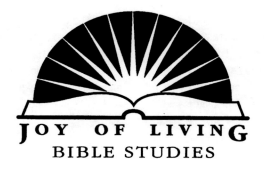

JOY OF LIVING
BIBLE STUDIES

Hebrews 7:23—8:13

It is impressive to see the earnestness of the writer of Hebrews as he sought to show his Jewish Christian brothers the wonders of God's grace. His consuming desire was that his readers' faith might be firmly established. He knew by experience that if they understood that God had set aside the types and shadows of Judaism in exchange for the reality of the Savior-hood and Priesthood of Christ, their love for the Lord would deepen. Their understanding of this "solid food" of the gospel would give them a new perspective on their redemption.

Christ gained our salvation by going to the cross (see 2 Corinthians 5:21). Now He guarantees our salvation by always living to intercede for us (see Hebrews 7:25). Have you come to God through faith in the Lord Jesus Christ? (See 2 Corinthians 5:17; 6:2.) If you have, Jesus Christ holds blessings from the Father with your name on them. These blessings He willingly gives to you as you pray for strength, encouragement, courage, patience, or whatever your daily needs may be! Where could you find a better model or better motivation to pray for your needs and others' needs today? Why not pause right now and take time to speak to the Father about these things?

A New Covenant

Hebrews 7:22 spoke of a "better covenant." This indicates that another covenant had existed before Christ came to earth. (The word "covenant" refers to a binding agreement or contract.) The prior covenant must have been good in some respects if the new one is "better." It was good because it served to restrain sin and to encourage godly living. Although not understood by all, it pointed to the coming of the Messiah.

At the Last Supper, Jesus gave the disciples broken bread and the cup, saying, "This cup is the new covenant in my blood, which is poured out for you" (Luke 22:20). The cup of His blood was poured out for the forgiveness of sins (see Matthew 26:28). Jesus is the guarantee of this better covenant. We receive all the benefits of it. We bear witness to it every time we take part in the sacrament of Holy Communion or the Eucharist, the remembrance feast (see 1 Corinthians 11:26).

The new covenant is permanent (see Hebrews 7:24); Christ pledged Himself to fulfill all it required. We who enjoy its blessings are enabled by the Holy Spirit to comply with its terms and to give obedi-

ence to the Lord (see Ephesians 3:16; Romans 8:11). Trying to please God under the laws of Judaism necessitated a continual "patching up" of imperfection. The Lord Jesus, our guarantee, makes us new creatures (see 2 Corinthians 5:17). He gives us spiritual life and light. He provides the power we need in order to live in accordance with the will of God. We will learn more about the old and new covenants in subsequent chapters of Hebrews.

This wonderful seventh chapter reaches its climax in the closing verses. With Christ appointed priest after the order of Melchizedek, the Levitical order was abolished, for the two could not function simultaneously. This change in the priesthood also superceded the entire ceremonial law, of which the Aaronic priesthood was the foundation. A new and better system was introduced, with a great high priest whose perfection secures forever the salvation of all who put their trust in Him.

Christ Intercedes for Us

The first word in Hebrews 7:25 refers to the previous statements about Jesus, "*Therefore* he is able to save completely those who come to God through him, because he always lives to intercede for them" (italics added). Jesus is able to save us completely because of the oath of His consecration, because God does not change His purposes, because of the better covenant which Jesus guarantees, and because His priesthood is permanent. Christ's power is limitless; He is all-sufficient and is completely capable of accomplishing His purposes (see Ephesians 3:20). When we receive Christ as Savior, we are saved from the penalty of sin (see John 5:24). Our loving God protects His children from Satan's onslaughts and saves us from the power of sin (see Romans 6:14). Jesus' final triumph will bring our deliverance from the presence of sin (see Revelation 21:3,27).

To be saved completely means that Christ will not begin a work in us and then leave us to our own devices (see 2 Corinthians 4:16; Philippians 1:6). His salvation is perfect and it is forever. Nothing is too hard for Him. Believers have all sorts of problems, opposition, and difficulties. Rest assured that no matter what may confront you, your great high priest is sufficient to cope with any trial, sorrow, disappointment or failure. Praise the Lord for such a Savior, for such a mediator! He saves those who come to God through faith in Him. We must come to Him in obedience and absolute dependence on the sufficiency of His sacrifice and His priestly office.

We know that sinners cannot be saved without the death of Christ. "For if, when we were God's enemies, we were reconciled to him through the death of his Son, how much more, having been reconciled, shall we be saved through his life!" (Romans 5:10). All praise to Him who by offering Himself secured forever our redemption. All praise to Him for always living to intercede for us. Christ intercedes so that nothing may separate His own from Him—neither "trouble or hardship or persecution or famine or nakedness or danger or sword" (Romans 8:35). As believers we continue to live in Satan's territory and are still tempted with the influences of the world; therefore, we need the priestly care of Christ. Through Him we are delivered from the enemy, given grace to meet every need, and kept in fellowship with the Father. Christ answers Satan's accusations against us. He keeps us day by day on our earthly pilgrimage and will at last set us in the presence of His glory without stain or wrinkle (see Ephesians 5:27).

Christ's Qualifications

Hebrews 7:26 outlines the qualifications of a high priest who would be suited to the needs of sinners. The first requirement is holiness, the separateness of belonging to God. He always pleased His Father and sought to do His will (see John 5:30; 6:38). Christ's conformity to God's will was evident in His relationships during His earthly life. He loved people and went about healing physical as well as spiritual ills. He never returned evil for evil. The great high priest must also be blameless and pure. Christ was undefiled by the sin around Him. Even His encounter with Satan left Him spotless (see Matthew 4:1-11). The statement that Christ was set apart from sinners summarizes what He is in Himself: holy and undefiled. It shows that He met all the requirements. After he accomplished His sacrifice, Christ was exalted above the heavens and was given the place of highest honor at God's right hand in the heavenly realms (see Ephesians 1:20-23), where He continues His high priestly ministry.

The Levitical high priest had to sacrifice for his own sins again and again (see Leviticus 4:3-12). On the Day of Atonement, he had to bring a sin offering for himself before he could present the offerings of the people (see Leviticus 16). His offering could not be included with theirs. But Christ, the perfect high priest, needed no sacrifice for Himself. Because His offering was perfect, there will never need to be another sacrifice for sin.

Jewish believers who remained steadfast in the traditions and ceremonies of Judaism found it difficult to bring themselves to accept the change to the new order of priesthood. They had to be persuaded that Christ had superseded the Levitical priesthood, since Christ was the Son of God, whereas the priests were mere men. The law had appointed as priests men who were weak; God's oath appointed the perfect Son of God. The Aaronic priests had sin; Christ had none. The service of the Levitical priests was temporary. Christ's is forever.

The Perfect Priest

You have no doubt discovered that the seventh and eighth chapters of Hebrews belong together. The sermon of the seventh chapter, based on Psalm 110:4, is summarized in chapter eight. The first verses point out that since Christ is seated at God's right hand, there is no doubt that He serves in the heavenly sanctuary, not in the earthly tabernacle or temple. In chapter seven, Christ's superb person is before us, while the eighth chapter speaks of His ministry.

"What we are saying" in Hebrews 8:1 refers to the whole letter of Hebrews. Specifically it may be applied to the section from 4:14 through chapter 7, the theme of which is the exalted Christ in His high priestly ministry. Jewish priests could not measure up to the qualifications that describe the Lord Jesus. He was holy, blameless, and exalted above the heavens. In every way, Christ surpasses the sons of Aaron.

One of the most notable contrasts between Christ and the Aaronic priesthood is seen in the offering of the high priest on the Day of Atonement. As indicated earlier, the priest took the blood of the sacrifice into the Holy Place. He passed beyond the curtain to the Most Holy Place. There he stood momentarily before the atonement cover above the Testimony, the symbolic meeting place with God, and sprinkled it with blood. His awesome duty completed, he immediately left that place, not to return until the next year. (See Leviticus 16.)

How different our blessed Lord, our high priest, is! After He offered Himself as a sacrifice to God, He entered heaven to sit at God's right hand in a joyous reunion that will last forever (see Mark 16:19). What a comfort this must have been to the Hebrew Christians whose unsaved friends may have harassed them for having no fellowship with the temple rites and ceremonies. The author of this letter reminds them that "we do have such a high priest" (Hebrews 8:1)—not an earthly one, but one who is eternal in heaven.

This very same high priest is the high priest of believers today. He is the mediator who pleads your case in the court of heaven. He anticipates your needs, temptations, and trials, and He intercedes even before you feel the buffeting of Satan. Before Peter's denial of Him, the Lord said, "Simon, Simon, Satan has asked to sift you as wheat. But I have prayed for you, Simon, that your faith may not fail. And when you have turned back, strengthen your brothers" (Luke 22:31-32). What an encouragement this is for us. Though Peter, who always seemed to speak out of turn, failed again and again, he did become a source of strength to his fellow believers. He faithfully witnessed to both Jews and Gentiles, and the Holy Spirit directed that his letters be preserved and included in our Bible. God's grace knows no limitation!

The writer of Hebrews sought to draw attention away from the earthly temple with its types and shadows to the reality of Christ. Jesus "serves in the sanctuary, the true tabernacle" (Hebrews 8:2), giving us access to God. The true sanctuary is in heaven where Christ Himself officiates. Israel's tabernacle symbolized the reality of the heavenly sanctuary. As Aaron presented the atoning blood of the sacrifice in the Most Holy Place, so Christ presented His shed blood in the presence of God. The true tabernacle is lasting, whereas the tabernacle of Israel was temporary. The force of the word "true" is seen in Christ's statement, "I tell you the truth, it is not Moses who has given you the bread from heaven, but it is my Father who gives you the true bread from heaven" (John 6:32).

When construction of the first tabernacle and its furnishings was about to begin, God warned Moses to make everything according to what had been shown him on Mount Sinai. Exactly what Moses saw is not certain. Did God reveal to His servant that the tabernacle represented Christ in His incarnation, His sacrifice, His priesthood and glorification? We don't know. But we can be certain that the entire service of sacrifices and offerings, earthly priests and altars, was designed to show us heavenly things, which have their fulfillment in the Lord Jesus.

Hebrews points out that if Christ had remained on earth, He could not have been a priest. The law governed the earthly priesthood with its offerings and ceremonies. Christ was not of the right tribe, and His offering was not as prescribed by the law. Christ offered Himself; He entered the heavenly sanctuary, the true Most Holy Place. Just as the high priests of old were required to complete the offering of the sacrifice by carrying the blood into the Most Holy Place, so Christ had to appear in the presence of God for us. This way the offering of Himself was made effective.

A New Relationship

You will recall from Lesson 2 the various covenants God has made with humanity. It was the last—the new covenant—that the writer described in Hebrews 8. A covenant is an agreement, and in the biblical sense, it is God who states the terms; we cannot change them, but must either accept or reject the offer. After the law was given to Moses, God offered Israel a special relationship to Himself, dependent solely on their obedience to the law. They accepted the terms of the covenant given at Mount Sinai, but God made it clear that the relationship would exist only as long as the people obeyed His commands. In contrast, our relationship to God today is based on grace through faith in Christ's death for us. On this basis, eternal life is unconditional. This covenant is, in effect, a will. By it we obtain an inheritance.

We have seen that the law and the old covenant were inadequate and so had to be abolished. The promise of a new covenant had been known for a long time. It was recorded by the prophet Jeremiah in Jeremiah 31:31-34 hundreds of years before these verses were quoted in Hebrews. Note that ultimately this covenant will bring together the ten tribes of Israel and the two tribes of Judah, which had been separated long before Jeremiah spoke his prophecy.

The kingdom of Israel had divided during King Rehoboam's reign (see 1 Kings 12). There were always those who strictly obeyed the ceremonial law. There were also those who did not observe the details of the law. But when the new covenant is written upon people's hearts, all shall know Him. Obedience to the Lord will be rendered in love rather than in fear of judgment. While God still exercises His justice, that justice is mingled with His love and grace. No longer must we try to satisfy God's requirements with gifts and sacrifices. Now it is all of God, who says, "I will be merciful—I will remember their sins no more."

The new covenant is based on the finished work of Christ, who said, "This is my blood of the covenant, which is poured out for many

for the forgiveness of sins" (Matthew 26:28; see also 1 Corinthians 11:25). It assures complete obliteration of sin. Believers now are beneficiaries of the blessings of redemption related to the new covenant. We take part in Christ and in the riches of our inheritance in Him.

Perhaps you have been trusting in your own "works" to earn your way into heaven. In God's sight, your righteousness is like filthy rags (see Isaiah 64:6). Put your trust in Christ's perfect righteousness and His all-sufficient, once-for-all sacrifice for your sin. If you do not have the peace of God and the assurance that your sins are put away forever, take the step of faith now. Make your peace with God (see Romans 5:1). If you have peace with God, how are you sharing your faith with others who desperately need to know Christ's forgiveness, peace, and love?

This study on Hebrews continues in Part 2. The Study Questions for Lesson 11 are at the beginning of Part 2.

Notes:

Notes:

Notes: